SORTED

'a recipe for student survival'

"A great example to other students and budding entrepreneurs to get out there with a worthwhile cause and make it sustainable through a commercial mindset."

SIR RICHARD BRANSON

"All the right ingredients for a winner, a good worthwhile idea, youth, passion and a well produced book, spot on for its audience."

DUNCAN BANNATYNE

"I think it's a great idea what you're doing... get out there and teach the young how to cook."

AINSLEY HARRIOTT

"SORTED is just what every student needs; straightforward, wholesome, foolproof and includes cheats to satisfy even the laziest cook."

THE TIMES

"The SORTED team have created a cooking bible for student life, it's humorous and informative."

THE SUN

"All singing, all dancing YouTube gurus who are intent on transforming our lives..."

THE GUARDIAN

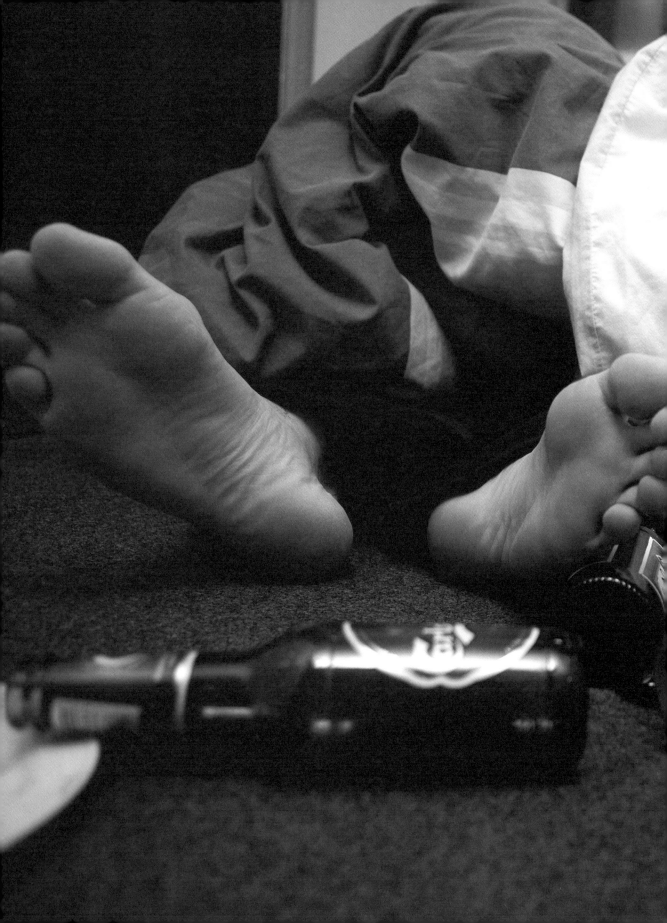

SORTED

'a recipe for student survival'

with recipes by Ben Ebbrell and photography by Barry Taylor
written by Steve Lau and **THE SORTED CREW**

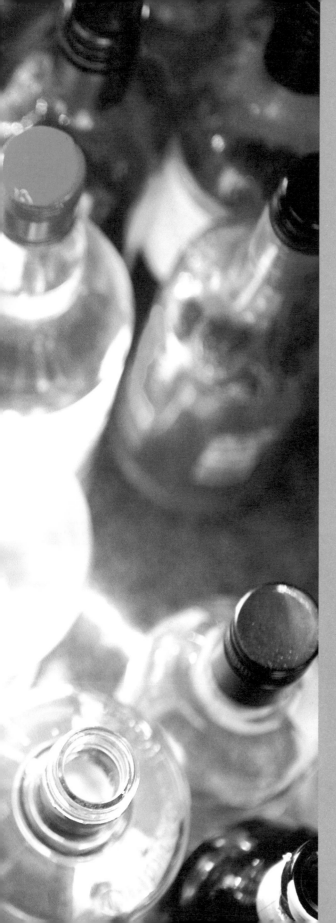

First published in 2009 by
Co-incidence Ventures Ltd

SORTED

'a recipe for student survival'

A CIP catalogue record for this book is available
from the British Library.

ISBN 978-0-9559408-1-1

Designed by Sharon Cluett
Edited by Aaron Brown

Printed and bound in China by
China Printing Solutions International.

visit us online at
www.sortedfood.com

See the crew in action on our downloadable videos,
keep yourself updated on all the latest tips and settle
in to the student community. Whether you've got a
sound piece of student advice, learnt a sneaky new trick
or have come up with a new recipe, visit our site and
make a post. Share your knowledge with fellow students
across the globe.

another Co-incidence.
www.Co-incidence.com

contents

introduction

There comes a time when every bird must fly the nest. For members of the **SORTED** team, that momentous day took place more than three years ago. After saying our final farewells to friends and family, we walked off into the sunset and into the next chapter of our lives... university!

The fun-filled days of play fighting in the common room, performing childish schoolboy pranks and displaying mischievous behaviour in the classroom were replaced with the hard knocks of real life – learning to survive without our mothers! Unfortunately for us, we hadn't listened to our parents' advice and we were adamant that living without them would be easy. Our first term at university proved us wrong and ringing home to beg for kitchen advice became the norm.

As veterans of what can be an inhospitable student war zone if you're not prepared for it, we have decided to combat this problem and lend a helping hand to the hundreds and thousands of freshers who each year venture off to university without our first-hand knowledge of what to expect. Combining our living-away-from-home expertise with our insatiable appetite for tasty grub, we have created what we consider to be the ultimate recipe for student survival. As a bonus we have garnished the book with a generous helping of top tips and 'did you know' snippets to prevent you experiencing domestic crises. The finished article is a student-friendly survival guide centered on healthy meals which are cheap (we provide guide prices per portion), classy and, most importantly, tasty!

Using our creative genius we present to you eight chapters of essential survival information. **The first move** guides you by the hand from the very moment you get your A-level results to taking your first few steps as a fresher... and beyond. Here, we cover the nooks and crannies in those months leading up to university, including a food shopping guide, a smattering of top tips and crucial items we recommend you pack. In chapter two, **filling up**, we preach a chorus of team spirit through cooking with friends. Next we introduce **fighting fit**, crammed full of healthy and energising dishes which are brilliant for giving groggy students the vital lift they need when times get tough. The action-packed and dangerously exciting nights out chapter hosts the best advice on making those social occasions events to remember! **Brain boosters** then brings you right back down to Earth by recommending all the best foods to feed your noggin and transform you into an exam-hungry fighting machine. In the sophisticated **meals to impress** chapter we take up the challenge of turning even the most inept student zombie into a domestic master chef via a brigade of modern recipes designed to blow the socks off 'that special person'. We then turn our attention to **odds & sods**, drawing together all the unplanned and crazy dishes you'll look to when forced to cook in a hurry. As if that's not enough, we finish by showcasing the first-class contributions we've received from students we've met along the way as the SORTED crew continues on **the mission** to challenge the student diet.

The creation of this project has brought us all back together and made us closer as a group. Through the bickering, banter and brilliance we are proud to present the bible of student living, which effortlessly educates the novice to the pro and ensures that university years – not school – are really the best of your life. Our wisdom and inside secrets will add value to your emotional rollercoaster of a journey and stop you from making the same mistakes we did, as well as having a laugh on the way.

So sit back, relax and enjoy **SORTED**, the recipe for student survival.

Jon Gavaghan

Barry Taylor

Jamie Spafford

Steve Lau

Tom Barnes

Ben Ebbrell

Richard Smith

Adam Wilkinson

the first move

You shake uncontrollably as you open the brown paper envelope and quickly scan the results. A sigh of relief follows as you realise your graft has paid off. After telling everyone from your aunt in Oz to the local kebab man, you finally crack open a beer and begin a session you'll never remember. Yep, it's results day – the only socially acceptable time to drink before midday.

The next day reality hits you with a thud. The confirmation letter from UCAS comes through and your uni attacks you with a wad of information. Your hangover worsens as you try and take it all in: fresher's week events, accommodation details, lecture timetables – the list seems endless. On top of this, you don't have a clue what stuff to pack and neither do your mates. Emotions run high as your mum suddenly realises her 'little cherub' is leaving the family home, while your dad is about as useful as a one-legged man in an arse kicking contest.

Soon, Tesco becomes a second home as your remaining days are spent raiding the homewares section and forking out for whacky kitchen appliances resembling sex toys. And don't even start on the food; you've bought so much that it makes you and your folks look like you're hoarding a house of illegal immigrants. So slow down and take a good read of this chapter. It's your student bible and will help you tackle this mess. We've included all the top tips and hints needed to prevent student meltdown and, more importantly, allow you more time to being a full-time socialite in that vital first week of uni.

the 'formal' stuff

It's boring but it has to be done: all the soul-destroying admin and packing you wish you could fob off to your personal assistant (if you could afford one) so that you'd have more time to do, erm, nothing. But life sucks, so chin up and let's wade through the stuff you need to do.

What to pack

Rain Man you are not. No normal kid can retain all that 'super-important' and mind-numbingly dull uni information in their heads. Not while you kill off your brain's grey matter on a weekly booze binge anyway. So make a list of what you need to take. Here's one we've conjured up to give you a rough idea.

Clothes
So you don't have to prance around like Adam and Eve.

Cleaning stuff
Okay, so we're not saying bring enough cleaning products to host a spring-clean party but bear in mind that some students live like scum. Without your mum to clean up after you it'll be wise to have some emergency kit for when you spill your TV dinner. So make sure you bring:
- Toilet/bathroom cleaner
- Wet wipes
- Odour eaters/air fresheners
- Febreze – to get rid of nasty whiffs from almost any material
- Upmarket washing-up liquid, eg Fairy

Washing stuff
Some students might look like tramps but you don't have to smell like one too.
- Your usual toiletries, eg toothbrush, deodorant, etc.
- Washing powder/tablets/liquid, eg Persil

Computer and printer
A crucial piece of kit which you'd struggle to live without.

Old and new textbooks
Dig out your A-level textbooks 'cos they might come in handy for your degree. And remember to buy the books your uni recommends. Get 'em cheap, of course.

Stationery equipment
We're not just talking about your bog standard pencil case itinerary here but also things such as memory sticks, blank CDs, Post-it Notes (for those with memories like goldfish), and so on.

Sports equipment
Taking an old football or tennis racket will allow you to show off that hidden talent you have for sports at your university club. Or it will make you red faced when you get thrashed by your mates. Nevertheless, it's all banter.

Kitchen utensils

Stuff your everyday kitchen novice will need:

- Small, medium and large saucepans
- Frying pan/wok
- Colander
- Chopping board
- Small prep knife, large knife and bread knife
- Bowls
- Baking tray
- Wooden spoon
- Fish slice
- Tin opener
- Bottle opener
- Ladle
- Cheese grater
- Sieve
- Cutlery – set of six (knife/fork/dessert spoon/ teaspoon)
- Crockery – set of four (main plate/tea plate/bowl)
- Glasses – set of two or four (tumbler/wine/pint)
- Tupperware containers – quality for fridge/freezer
- Tea towels x 2
- Dishcloths/scourers/J cloths

TOP TIP

First impressions count. Your credibility, reputation and image will all be decided within the first couple of weeks. So don't be the embarrassing drunk who's remembered for streaking down the hallway at 3am. Unless everyone else is doing it of course.

Kitchen equipment – group purchases

Don't buy this gear until you've seen what's provided in your halls of residence and met your housemates. Then trek together to the local supermarket or Argos in your first week and chip in for the team equipment. Split the cost between a group of five or six and it works out a bargain:

- Toaster
- Kettle
- Microwave
- Food processor or stick blender
- Cheap set of kitchen scales
- Draining rack for sink
- Iron (and board if not provided)

remember or else!

Don't endure an 'oh no' moment. Definition: when you realise you have just forgotten something very important. So save yourself a long journey back home and follow our tips:

Take all important documents with you – such as the letters from your uni and UCAS confirming your place, accommodation details, your loan correspondence from the Student Loans Company, insurance stuff, National Insurance card, NHS details (available from your GP) and bank information.

Check all your info before you go – re-read all correspondence you've had from your uni and remind yourself what you need on the day before you leave. Check the uni forums online to keep updated.

Bring an address book – old-fashioned but a life-saver if you ever lose your phone on a night out.

Take your mobile phone with you – you'll be needing it a lot in the first week to sort your life out.

Don't forget spare passport photos – essential for those wads of forms you'll be filling in, including your NUS card.

TOP TIP

First day + open door = friendly student. Be this student. Keep your door open in that vital first week. Invest in a doorstop and use it.

As soon as you arrive

The more organised you are before you arrive, the more free time you'll have to chill out with your new mates. Try to get there as early as possible to sort this lot out and avoid the rush of other students:

Registration – sign up for your course, get keys for accommodation. Seems obvious but many students forget.

Money – check your loan has arrived. This will be your financial lifeline during the first year.

Tuition fees – make sure the uni has all your details on how you're gonna pay your fees. Whether you're jammy enough to get sponsorship or are leeching off the Student Loans Company, it's worth checking that both your uni and the fee-paying saviours have your details on file.

Accommodation fees – again, this should be settled once you register.

Register with a new GP – fill in the forms and sign up to your local surgery. Will be crucial when you need some pills for fresher's flu.

NUS/library card – pick these up ASAP 'cos once you have 'em they make you an official student!

Bus passes – if you have to regularly travel in for your lectures, it's gonna be cheaper to get a bus pass. Ask at your student union about how it all works.

Buy a TV licence – if you have a TV or TV equipment in your room (think PCs with broadcast cards) then you are legally required to buy a TV licence. Don't try and chance it 'cos the TV licence people do regular checks in halls and, if caught, you'll find your pocket a grand lighter. For communal areas with a TV, such as the kitchen, share the cost with your flatmates.

Change of address – let everyone back home know so they can send you good old-fashioned letters!

Sort your room out – okay, this ain't majorly important but it will help you when you stumble back leathered after your first night out and find your room is a bombsite.

The big food shop

Don't let your parents sneak away until they do a big shop for you. You'll be tempted to buy convenience food that's quick and easy, but be warned, it won't last and will be pricey. Take our advice and shop smart with these long-lasting shelf items. Buy these along with your usual stuff and it'll stretch your food much further:

Cupboard food
- Pasta, rice, Smash powder sachets, noodles, couscous
- Salt and pepper mills
- Cooking oil (vegetable)
- Stock cubes
- Collection of common spices, including cumin, chilli powder, cinnamon, paprika, coriander
- Mustard
- Jam
- Marmite
- Peanut butter
- Sauce sachets – cheese, fajita mix, hollandaise
- Tinned chopped tomatoes
- Tinned beans – various, including kidney, butter, haricot
- Tinned tuna
- Baked beans
- Tinned soups
- Tinned fruit – desperate last-minute supply
- Tea
- Coffee
- Sugar
- Ketchup/BBQ sauce
- Dried fruit and nuts
- Cornflakes/muesli

Freezer stash
- Oven chips
- Frozen peas
- Sausages
- Loaf of sliced bread
- Kievs/pies/quiche – then at least there's always an option for dinner
- Minced beef

the aftermath...

Once you've settled in, see off your folks, dry the tears and get a group together for a wander around campus and town. Places to visit include:

The union – your definite first stop. Rummage around the stalls picking up freebies, sign up for a bunch of stuff and ensure you know what's on that week.

Campus – take a nosey round the buildings you'll be having your lectures and seminars in so you can get your bearings 'cos it's likely the next time you're trying to find them you'll be running late.

Halls events/socials – any credible hall will have themed nights, balls and sports events throughout the year. Sign up for them as there's always banter to be had. If no-one else is sorting something, take the initiative and set up some events with mates.

Public transport hot spots – unless you have a car, buses and trains will be your main mode of transport to get out and about. Invest in a 16-25 Railcard. It'll save you money in the long term. Check out the local timetables and routes. No-one forgets the hero who remembers when the last bus leaves after a night out in town.

The local area – find out where your local grocers, supermarkets and restaurants are. Grab a map of your new local area, lose yourself in some tucked-away alleys and you might just find a quality student pub lurking there.

Now what?

You've drunk like a fish and that first week is over. Time to pick up the pieces. You're getting a little homesick while trying to settle in at the same time. Cosy up and read our advice for the next steps:

Jobs – if you're after an extra bit of cash to tide you over, part-time jobs are always on offer somewhere. Ask at your union bar, library, as well as signing up to a job agency. Scan the local paper too and don't forget to update your CV!

Budgets – you've just blown a month's budget in a week. You laugh hysterically 'cos it's the only thing stopping you from crying. Don't fret, start that budget again and keep a diary of your costs. If things do spiral out of control there's always sound advice available at the student union where you can apply for hardship funds, bursaries and emergency loans.

Help and guidance – you're in a Catch-22 situation because you need some advice but think your new mates might laugh at you. Whether it's a sexual, job-related or university problem you can get in touch with the lovely people at Nightline, a support service run for students by students. Contact details will be available from the student union.

Keep your head up and suck it all in – this will probably be the first time you've lived away from home and it's time to step up to the mark and be independent. Stay ahead of the game and in control of your commitments. Print out lecture timetables, keep tabs on all the activities the sports clubs and societies you've joined are running and save just a little time to do some work, but above all else – have a laugh!

RECIPES

* DIY chicken fajitas

* rustic bean and sausage stew

* chicken, mushroom and tarragon pasta bake

* one pot wonder —
leek and bacon risotto

* cheats' fish pie

* beef meatballs in tomato sauce

filling up

Your first university lesson: learn to share. Students do a lot of sharing. Soon you'll be sharing milk (maybe without your consent, initially), drink, cigarettes and – if you get lucky – sexual activity. So why not go the whole hog and share food as well? There's nothing better than when the lads return from Asda after a hunter-gatherer session only for the girls to work their David Blaine-like magic to transform the food into an extravagant feast. Any chance to get stuck in and share a truckload of nosh while taking the mick out of each other's culinary skills is a dead cert for creating unforgettable banter.

This chapter has been designed to ease you in gently and guide you by the hand in producing some really great meals. From simple no-fuss wraps to tasty homemade stews that even Mr Bean could blag. So gather round your mates and tuck into quality food fit to stoke the stomachs of even the most ravenous students.

And remember, keep an eye on our website at www.sortedfood.com for more great recipes.

DIY chicken fajitas

At uni, the kitchen will be a big social jungle. It will be populated by a range of different species: the kid who survives off oven/microwave meals, the culinary genius who claims she can't cook, and the lads who live on takeaways. So what better way to bring everyone together than with these DIY fajitas.

The idea's simple – drum up a range of different fillings, lay 'em on your table and share the love.

2 chicken breasts
large onion
red pepper
yellow pepper
cajun spice mix (30g sachet)
8 flour tortilla wraps
pot each of salsa, guacamole and sour cream
bowl of crisp salad leaves

TOP TIP

Eating fajitas can get messy. Best to pile the food into the centre of the wrap then turn up the bottom before folding in each side.

strip raw chicken as thinly as possible.
slice peppers and onion.
fry chicken with onions in large saucepan or wok over very high heat for 5 minutes.
add peppers and continue to fry for another 5 minutes.
sprinkle over the Cajun spice mix and toss together.
warm tortillas in the microwave for a few seconds.
lay out all fillings on the table and dive in to make your own before everyone beats you to it.

serves ❹
£2.20 per portion
10 mins prep ■ 15 mins cooking

rustic bean and sausage stew

The phone rings... it's that call you've been dreading all week. It's your mum, aka the Spanish Inquisition of the cooking world. She wants to know what you've been eating, whether you've been eating at sensible times and checking you're not making too much of a disgrace of your liver through heavy drinking.

Don't fret, simply inform her that you and your flatmates will be avoiding the perils of drink and are staying in to 'revise' while eating a hearty meal of stew. As quick as a takeaway, half the price and with a fraction of the calories. Students, please form an orderly queue...

shot of olive oil

8 decent sized sausages

medium onion

stick of celery

carrot or two

tsp fresh or dried oregano

3 cloves of garlic

3 different tins of beans, eg kidney, butter, haricot

tin of chopped tomatoes

handful of fresh parsley

grill sausages under high heat until golden.

dice carrot, celery, onion and garlic and fry in oil for 10 minutes using large pan.

drain beans, tip contents into pan along with chopped tomatoes and oregano.

chop cooked sausages into chunks and stir into bean mix.

simmer for 10 minutes – chop parsley while you wait.

sprinkle with parsley just before serving.

serves **4**
£1.20 per portion
10 mins prep ■ 20 mins cooking

chicken, mushroom and tarragon pasta bake

Drinking initiations... we all have to face them some time or another. Whether it's for your sports team, a society do or a kitchen social, they're potentially devastating rituals which will make you more anxious than a pig attending a bacon convention. So save face and remember to line your stomach well beforehand.

This quick pasta bake does just the job. Good old-fashioned stodgy munch which will slow down alcohol absorption and make you look like a seasoned pro in the shot-slurping stakes...

2 chicken breasts

tin of cream of chicken and mushroom soup

clove of garlic

breakfast bowl of button mushrooms

handful of fresh tarragon

penne pasta (400g)

handful of grated cheese

knob of butter

shot of olive oil

boil pasta in salted water until cooked – see packet for cooking time.

crush garlic and slice the mushrooms.

fry garlic and mushrooms in a little oil and the butter.

drain pasta when cooked.

cut chicken into strips and add to mushrooms.

pour in soup.

heat to a simmer and cook for 5 minutes.

stir through finely chopped tarragon once chicken is cooked.

mix in cooked pasta as well.

turn out into oven-proof casserole dish.

sprinkle with grated cheese and bake at 200°C until crisp and golden on top.

serves **4**
£1.20 per portion
5 mins prep ■ 15 mins cooking ■ 15 mins baking

buddy up with a mate
when cooking and cleaning –

it's a lot cheaper!

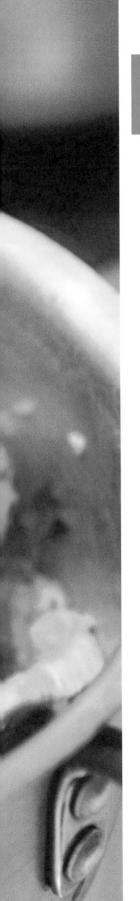

one pot wonder - leek and bacon risotto

Dirty plates lead to rotting food, which leads to bad hygiene, which leads to death. Okay, so we may have exaggerated here. But our point is every student hates cleaning. We all want minimum effort with maximum result, and this dish does it all. Bung everything into one pot and that's your lot. Simple, wholesome food that's like a slap in the face for all those hard-core kitchen grafters.

shot of olive oil
large leek
bacon offcuts (750g)
mushrooms (400g)
2 cloves of garlic
⅓ of a bottle of white wine
just over a litre of chicken stock
risotto rice (500g)
cream cheese (200g)
handful of chopped parsley

shred leek and wash thoroughly.

sweat leek in a pan in the shot of oil with the lid on.

crush garlic and add to leek.

remove excess fat from bacon and cut into bite-sized pieces.

add to leek mix and continue to fry.

slice mushrooms and chuck them in.

pour rice in and stir to evenly coat grains.

slosh in the wine and stir until nearly absorbed.

ladle in stock bit by bit, stirring throughout until rice is plump and cooked (approximately 20 minutes).

stir in the cream cheese, parsley and season.

serve in bowls. Perfect for TV dinners with mates.

serves **6**
£1.40 per portion
10 mins prep ■ 30 mins cooking

Don't season until tasting — bacon can be naturally very salty.

cheats' fish pie

For any student, the mention of cooking a pie sounds like hard work. But we've created some clever shortcuts to this usually costly and 'it's a waste of my time' dish. You don't have to be Delia to make this one: the seafood chowder acts as a great ready-made sauce, while that stale loaf in your cupboard will double up as a quality mashed potato substitute which will crisp up a treat. Carefully slide out of the oven when golden and splodge onto a plate for your savagely hungry friends.

bag of frozen white fish fillets (800g)
6 eggs
large onion
2 tins of seafood chowder soup
2 large fistfuls of fresh spinach
¾ loaf of stale sliced white bread
knob of butter
shot of olive oil

TOP TIP
Economy food is the way forward. Dont be ashamed when the greasy 17-year-old checkout worker looks down on your Smart Price bread or Value eggs. They'll be doing the same next year once they've ragged their overdraft.

hard-boil the eggs in salted boiling water for 6-7 minutes then refresh/cool them under cold running water.

dice onion finely and sweat in a little oil in large saucepan.

tip in both tins of soup once onion is soft and heat through.

skin and roughly chop fish fillets into large pieces.

wash spinach and add to soup with fish.

shell and halve eggs. Stir into soup.

remove crusts from bread and cube it.

pour contents of pan into oven-proof dish and top with chopped bread.

dot with small knobs of butter and bake at 180°C until crisp and golden.

serves ⑥
£1.40 per portion
10 mins prep ■ 15 mins cooking ■ 15 mins baking

beef meatballs in tomato sauce

Minced beef– a staple in every student's fridge. So if you're fed up of the same old spag bol or cottage pie, then spice things up and try this tasty little number. Nuggets of meat swimming in a freshly made tomato sauce, which is great for dolloping out to your new found flatmates. A family favourite with a cutting edge.

meatballs
minced beef (approx 1.5 kg)
onion
4 cloves of garlic
2 large red chillies
fistful of fresh parsley
tbsp ground coriander
tbsp ground cumin
tbsp salt
2 eggs

tomato sauce
large onion
3 cloves of garlic
2 tins of chopped tomatoes
handful of fresh basil
dash of balsamic vinegar

dried pasta, depending on how hungry you are (600g)

dice the onion and garlic for the tomato sauce and sweat in a pan with little oil until soft.

tip in the chopped tomatoes and simmer for 20 mins.

chop the onion, garlic and chillies for the meatballs as fine as possible.

dump into big bowl with minced beef.

crack in the eggs and sprinkle over the spices, chopped parsley and salt.

beat together with your hands – get stuck in.

roll into small balls and fry in hot oiled pan until brown on all sides.

boil the pasta in salted water for 10-12 mins (see packet) and drain.

cut the basil and add to sauce with dash of vinegar, salt and pepper.

stir meatballs through the sauce to heat up again and serve mixed into the pasta with a sprinkling of cheese.

serves **6**
£1.60 per portion
15 mins prep ■ 25 mins cooking

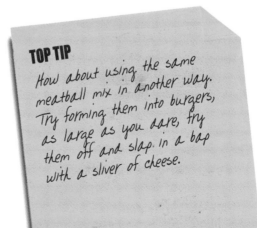

TOP TIP
How about using the same meatball mix in another way. Try forming them into burgers, as large as you dare, fry them off and slap in a bap with a sliver of cheese.

tips and tricks

Invest in a stupid amount of staple products such as pasta and rice. And when we say *invest* we mean buy it like it's going out of fashion. This stuff is like war-rationing food; it'll keep forever and is student cheap.

Economy is the way forward. Make the most of cheap supermarket brands with all the food basics. But, WARNING! Washing-up liquid is one item you can't skimp on – the expensive stuff lasts longer.

Your parents are a walking ATM. When they visit you at uni, cue the puppy dog eyes and freeload your way to an all-you-can carry supermarket trip.

Buddy up with a mate when cooking and cleaning. It's cheaper, will split the workload and make the kitchen a hoot.

Bread is freezable! So when you realise your loaf is on its sell-by date sling it in the freezer and have it as toast for breakfast instead.

Master the art of the late shop. Head down to the supermarket at 8pm to discover discounted fruit, vegetable, meat and bread bargains. Bonus!

Got the munchies and need a quick fix? Slot some frozen waffles or fish fingers into the toaster and they'll cook perfectly in no time. Job well done.

Keep it clean. If you're fortunate enough to have cleaners in your halls, make sure you befriend them like they are surrogate mothers. Shower them with (affordable) gifts, learn their first names and get some friendly banter going. Ultimately these lovely ladies are the ones sorting out the disgraceful mess you make!

Never turn down anything that's free. It doesn't matter if you don't want or need it – it's free! Prime pickings for freebies can be found at the union on fresher's stalls. You might be able to pick up enough free chocolate and drinks to last you your first week.

House rules

If you're one of the lucky few who has total trust in the others you share your kitchen with then consider yourself a rarity. The rest of us poor souls will more than likely have our milk, butter, bread or eggs nicked on a regular basis. Never take this personally, it happens. One way to prevent this is to set up ground rules when you move in. Alternatively, share your food with a mate... it's easy to steal off one student but to steal off two is a bigger guilt trip, plus they might just get their comeuppance when you get your mitts on 'em.

RECIPES

* portuguese soup

* moroccan carrot salad

* trio of houmus with crisp pitta dunkers

* oaty apple shake

* chicken, fennel and thyme casserole

* cajun spiced salmon, mango salsa and sweet potato chips

* raspberry and almond crumble

fighting fit

Remember getting up dead early as a kid on Saturday mornings and switching on the box to watch *Live & Kicking*? Children had it so easy back then. Fast-forward to today and you'll find that those same angelic kids have turned into walking zombies, hell-bent on procrastination and infecting the world with 'lazy syndrome', sneered at by their parents' generation as a taint on the *Homosapien* species. Which zoo are these animals kept in, we hear you ask? Well, brace yourself and find your nearest mirror, 'cos believe it or not as a student you'll find that you've morphed perfectly into our idle stereotype. Taking granny naps and walking around with cans of Red Bull on drip become common practice as you engage in a desperate attempt to make it through the day. The curse of aging has sapped your energy levels, puberty has made a joke of your face and a poor uni diet will shoot your immune system to pieces.

Wipe that tear off your cheek. The Elephant Man got over it and so can you. We've done all the hard work for you and concocted the most amazing dishes that will get you looking fit and feeling on top form again. So before you concede defeat and order the Stairlift 3000 Deluxe, glance over this next chapter and feel born again.

And remember, keep an eye on our website at www.sortedfood.com for more great recipes.

portuguese soup

A simple soup, jam-packed with goodness and boasting all the creature comforts of home cooking. It's a filling bit of broth and makes a quality lunch, or even enough for dinner for you and a few mates. Go on, take on the challenge of a Portuguese meal for four!

chorizo sausage (200g)
2 big potatoes
large onion
big bag of kale (200g)
3 cloves of garlic
litre of cold water
pinch of salt
pinch of smoked paprika
shot of olive oil

peel and roughly chop onion, potatoes and garlic.
chop chorizo.
throw onions into a deep pan with the shot of olive oil.
fry for 5 minutes on medium heat until soft and clear.
chuck in garlic and chorizo, cook for a couple of minutes to release flavours.
pour in litre of cold water and potatoes, bring to boil and simmer.
wash and chop kale while potatoes cook. After 15 minutes add kale to the potatoes.
boil for a further 3 minutes.
blitz in blender until smooth then return to pan. Thin down with a mug of water.
season to taste with salt and a sprinkle of smoked paprika.
mop up with crusty bread.

serves ❹
£0.80 per portion
5 mins prep ■ 25 mins cooking

moroccan carrot salad

That old wive's tale about carrots helping you see in the dark isn't entirely off target; they're packed with betacarotene, which is an important nutrient in maintaining healthy eyes. So wolf down this lovely little salad and you'll be able to find your way back from the student union post-skinful under the cover of darkness without having to cling to the walls to guide you.

2 large carrots
fistful of black pitted olives
8 red radishes
clove of garlic
lemon
clump of fresh parsley
½ tsp paprika
¼ tsp ground cumin
pinch of cinnamon
pinch of cayenne pepper
shot of olive oil

peel and quarter carrots lengthways, thinly slice into segments and throw into a bowl.

slice radishes and add to carrots.

quarter olives, chop parsley and combine with carrots.

whisk juice of lemon, oil and spices together with crushed garlic and dress the salad bits.

serve with mixed leaf salad and crusty bread for lunch or to accompany lamb or fish for dinner to whet any student's appetite.

serves **4**
£0.40 per portion
10 mins prep

trio of houmus with crisp pitta dunkers

Remember those Greek gods and goddesses you studied in school? The ones with bodies so taut and ripped you could cut your finger on one of their six-packs? Well this is the sort of munch they ate to give them such stunning figures. To them, houmus with pitta was the Greek version of what us Brits call beans on toast – low in fat and chock-full of protein and fibre. This dish can act as a quick and easy pre-lecture lunch or even a healthy snack to be prepped before the Hollyoaks omnibus. And you can't beat making your own houmus.

tin of chickpeas (400g)

lemon

clove of garlic

shot of olive oil

salt and pepper

Vary the recipe, add the following:
- **tsp ground cumin/½ tsp chilli powder**
or
- **tbsp red pesto**
or
- **zest of lime/tbsp coriander**

drain chickpeas and empty into food processor.

squeeze in juice of lemon.

crush clove of garlic and add to the mix.

blitz until a smooth paste.

season with salt and pepper and divide into 3 bowls.

beat a variety of ingredients into the separate bowls.

crisp the pitta breads in the toaster and cut into dunking strips.

enjoy as a casual lunch or for a healthier option to pre-dinner nibbles.

serves ❷
£1.00 per portion
10 mins prep

oaty apple shake

Okay, so we know what you're thinking. This resembles something you might see splattered on a pavement the morning after a heavy night, scooped up with a fork and garnished with an apple slice. But please, don't give your verdict until you try this shake. This is a guaranteed winner for those health-conscious athletes or dedicated detoxers. A hybrid smoothie and porridge breakfast, it provides all the good stuff you need when rushing that last-minute deadline or rising early for that all-important sporting fixture. This shake was just made for students...

4 cooking apples
½ tsp of cinnamon
zest of ½ a lemon
4 tbsp brown sugar
8 tbsp porridge oats
dollop of natural yoghurt (150g)
just over a pint of semi-skimmed milk (600ml)

core, peel and slice apples.
stew in pan with sugar, cinnamon and zest for 10 minutes.
cool the apple pulp.
toast oats in dry pan.
blend apple, oats, milk and yoghurt until desired consistency.
pour into glass, enjoy and you're ready to take on the world.

serves ❹
£0.60 per portion
5 mins prep ■ 10 mins cooking ■ allow time to cool

TOP TIP

By all means cheat and buy a jar of apple sauce. Not just ideal for roast pork but perfect for this too. Simply stir the cinnamon and sugar into the pre-cooked apple sauce.

chicken, fennel and thyme casserole

You are what you eat. Eat a pizza seven days a week and you'll have a face like one. Let's see you pull now... being able to cut shapes on the dance floor like John Travolta is no good if you need to wipe down every five minutes. Save face and do the groundwork to avoid this by eating well. The fennel in this idiot-proof dish is brilliant for skincare, containing active spot-preventing agents.

2 chicken breasts

courgette

2 handfuls of new potatoes

red onion

bulb of fennel

2 cloves of garlic

few sprigs of fresh thyme

shot of olive oil

large glass of white wine (250ml)

lemon

preheat oven to 200°C.

wash new potatoes and boil in salted water for 12-15 minutes.

crush garlic into roasting tray, add the ripped thyme before drizzling with oil.

lay chicken breasts in tray, rub oil into flesh and season.

halve fennel and then cut each half into thirds.

chop courgette and red onion into wedges.

scatter chopped vegetables around chicken.

lubricate all ingredients in oil and roast for 15 minutes.

crank up the temperature as high as it will go and slosh the wine into the tray.

add in juice from lemon.

roast for further 15 minutes and serve with buttered new potatoes.

serves ❷
£2.60 per portion
10 mins prep ■ 35 mins cooking

cajun spiced salmon, mango salsa and sweet potato chips

SAD. Students, learn this term. It stands for Seasonal Affective Disorder and apparently causes depression during winter. If you find anyone in this state, please consult this dish as it's the ultimate remedy. This meal is so charismatic, cheerful and chirpy it looks like it's come singing and dancing straight from the Caribbean. An extremely useful culinary weapon to rustle up when you next see your mate sulking, saying they're staying in 'cos of winter blues.

4 fresh salmon fillets

2 large sweet potatoes

shot of olive oil

sprinkle of cajun spice mix

salt and pepper

mango

3 tomatoes

2 spring onions

½ red onion

fistful of fresh coriander

fresh red chilli

2 limes

cut the potatoes into chunky slices (leave the skin on).

toss into a baking tray with the oil and season with salt and pepper.

roast wedges at 200°C for 30 mins.

dust salmon with Cajun spice mix and rub into flesh.

leave to marinate.

peel mango and roughly chop with spring onions, tomatoes, red onion and coriander.

combine all chopped ingredients with finely diced chilli and juice of 1 lime.

leave the mango salsa on the side while the rest of the meal cooks.

push the wedges to one side of the tray and slap the salmon fillets on the other.

return to oven for 15 mins or so until salmon is cooked.

pile the salsa onto plates, top with salmon fillet, wedge of lime and serve with sweet potato chips.

serves ❹
£2.80 per portion
20 mins prep ■ 45 mins cooking

NOTE
Sweet potato chips are tricky to get crispy without a mega hot oven. But they taste darn good regardless.

are you up for it?
let's get sorted!

raspberry and almond crumble

Okay, so we have a confession. Throughout the book we've been subtly trying to transform you from a student bum into a culinary genius by introducing no-brainer nosh that would put your mum's cooking to shame. And this one just might. Our version of this classic type of pud is rigged with a stunning combination of fruit designed to implode in your mouth, all topped off with a devastating crumble. When you go home, impress your family with this effortless dessert.

punnet of fresh raspberries (250g)

large orange

plain flour (100g)

diced cold butter (50g)

flaked almonds (50g)

caster sugar (50g + 1 tbsp)

tip raspberries into bowl.

grate over orange zest and add 1 tablespoon of caster sugar.

mix and divide into 4 oven-proof serving bowls or one large dish.

sieve flour into another bowl and rub butter into flour with fingertips until it resembles breadcrumbs.

stir through remaining sugar.

toast almonds in a dry pan until golden and add to crumble mix.

sprinkle crumble mix over raspberries to cover them.

bake at 180°C for 20 minutes.

serve with lashings of cream, ice cream or custard.

serves ❹
£1.00 per portion
10 mins prep ■ 20 mins cooking

tips and tricks

Mum knows best... wrong! When it comes to cleaning your glad rags toss EVERYTHING into the washing machine at 30°C. No need to separate your colours, whites and gut-wrenchingly smelly undercrackers. A hassle-free job unless you've got some serious stains to shift, eg bodily fluids, snakebite or chilli sauce from last night's kebab...

Tough-to-shift stains. Vanish Oxi Action will sort out the embarrassing marks your standard 30°C wash won't. A smart investment.

A breath of fresh air. Febreze. An odour-busting life-saver in a bottle. Spray it like a fireman all over your disgraceful smelling tops when you've forgotten to chuck 'em in the washer the night before. Your date will never know...

Join the gym. It'll be the cheapest membership you ever pay and keeping fit will give you more energy midweek for lectures (stop laughing, you'll need to go to at least one a week) and general physically demanding student antics.

Sign up with the campus doctor. Even if only for the free condoms they hand out.

Buy some wet wipes. The superheroes of the tissue world and the festival-goer's favourite. Pre-loaded with an army of bacteria-killings chemicals, they're good for cleaning up spillages or addressing any personal hygiene issues when you've no time for a shower.

Keep a supply of toilet paper in your room . It's not good when essentials get used up quickly, especially when you're caught short!

Rule no.1 — Look good and the rest will follow.

RECIPES

* chicken quesadilla

* citrus cocktail & tricky's fruit punch

* sorted top 5 drinking games

* beef and spinach curry

* breakfast 'soothie'

* sausage and mushroom tortilla

* banana bread

* cherry and almond muffins

nights out

Getting that first date. Seeing your lecturer walk into a door. Finding a quid on the union floor. All causes for celebration. However, before you bring that alcohol to your lips, remember drinking on an empty stomach is like laughing in your liver's face; he'll not be impressed and will pack up and leave before you can say "cirrhosis". So show him some love and keep the little chap happy by combining your drinking with some tasty grub. Our repertoire of stomach-lining recipes includes dishes great for pre-drinking, late-night munchies and curing hangover blues. They're tasty, wholesome and quick to prepare to boot.

Once you've had a good feed you're going to need to play some awesome drinking games to really get the night off to a flyer. We've searched the student grapevine to provide you with all the games a novice needs to know. So whether it be the legendary *Touch the Cup* or the more extreme death game of *Arrogance*, you'll soon leave your mates behind and become the Jedi knight of the drinking world. Read on... if you think you can handle it.

And remember, keep an eye on our website at www.sortedfood.com for more great recipes.

chicken quesadilla

Little cheesy thing. Three words which when muttered from a girl's mouth will crush any man's ego. However, it is also the literal Spanish translation for a quesadilla (pronounced kay-sar-dee-ah) – a panini-style Tex-Mex dish. Makes great party finger food, hot or cold. Quesadillas will also do wonders in building your street-cred as the next Gordon Ramsay of the student world. So, at university, where image and reputation is everything, this dish says it all... Casual, cool and slick. Just don't let it slip that the dish's name really means *shrivelled Wotsit* in Mexican.

chicken breast

cajun spice mix

red pepper

fistful of coriander

red onion

bag of grated mozzarella cheese

fresh red chilli

8 flour tortillas

dip of your choice – salsa/ guacamole/sour cream

slice chicken as thinly as possible.

spice chicken with Cajun spice mix, rubbing into the meat.

sizzle marinated chicken in a hot, oiled pan to cook through.

cut onion, pepper and chilli into thin strips.

lay half the tortillas out and sprinkle with grated cheese.

scatter onion, pepper and chilli slices over the cheese.

tear coriander leaves and sprinkle on top of onion, pepper and chilli.

divide the cooked chicken pieces between the 4 tortillas and finish with the leftover cheese.

put the remaining tortillas on top and fry in medium heat pan with spot of oil until crisp and golden.

quarter into portions and serve with preferred dip.

serves ❹
£1.00 per portion
10 mins prep ■ 10 mins cooking

citrus cocktail

Cocktail. The 1988 movie which catapulted Tom Cruise's silky shakin' skills onto the bar scene. Smooth, cool and collected, he scored a bunch of beauties, so which man wouldn't want to be blessed with his magic hands? Well, never fear, we've given you the opportunity to recreate this famous scene and dazzle your flatmates with half the effort. Remember that this is as fun to make as it is to swig.

lime

lemon

orange

tin of pineapple (in syrup)

glass of orange juice (200ml)

healthy splash of vodka

handful of ice cubes

halve citrus fruits.

squeeze into blender (try to avoid pips).

empty pineapple into blender.

crush ice and add to the mix with orange juice.

splash in a 'responsible' measure of vodka.

blitz to a slushy texture.

pour into glass and finish with lime zest.

tricky's fruit punch

Move aside Lambrini and White Lightning cider, 'Tricky' otherwise known as Richard (our very own social sec) has created the new pre-going out beverage in town. Oh yes, that's right, this citrus cocktail is one hell of a sophisticated concoction that thrusts a little *Sex and the City* culture back into scummy student life. If you're sipping this with the girls or 'manning up' with the lads, mooch around and get people to chip in for the alcohol, throw together and enjoy whilst playing every drinking game under the sun. Tasty, sweet and best of all, idiot proof.

litre of vodka

litre of Malibu/coconut flavoured rum

3 litres of orange juice

2 litres of cranberry juice

swirl the alcohol into the bottom of a bowl/bucket.

pour in the fruit juices.

stir well.

dump bowl/bucket in the middle of the drinking circle.

ladle into glasses.

NO student egos were harmed in the making of this video.

SORTED top 5 drinking games

⑤ boat race

You need
- Two even-numbered teams
- Alcohol of choice

The set-up
Players are divided into two teams and then sit one behind another on the floor in two parallel rows.

Game play
Once everyone is seated nominate someone to start the race with "Racers ready! Three... two... one... drink!" Then the first racers, sat at the front of each team, quaff their drinks as quickly as possible. The first to completely finish their drink puts the empty glass/bottle upside down on their head. The second racer then starts their drink. The race continues in this manner until all players have finished. The first team to do so wins.

④ screw the dealer

You need
- A minimum of 4 players
- Alcohol of choice
- A table everyone can sit round
- A deck of playing cards

The set-up
Everyone sits in a circle with their drink and each player is dealt a card. The player with the lowest card (ace low/king high) is initially designated as the dealer. All cards are returned to the dealer. The cards from one suit are then removed from the deck and placed in order, face-up across the table. The remaining cards are shuffled.

Game play
The dealer asks the first player on their left to guess the value (from ace to king) of the card on top of the deck. The dealer peeks to see if they are right. If the first guess is correct then the dealer drinks three gulps of alcohol. If the first guess is wrong then the dealer truthfully tells the player whether the card is higher or lower than their guess. The player then guesses again and the dealer places the card face up on the table on top of the corresponding number of the previously discarded suit.

If the second guess is correct then the dealer drinks two gulps of alcohol. If the second guess is wrong then the player drinks the same number of gulps of alcohol equal to the difference between their second guess and the value of the card.

Play moves to the next person and continues this way in a clockwise fashion until the deck is exhausted.

Once three players have failed to guess the top card correctly on either guess then the player to the left of the dealer becomes the dealer.

3 pub golf

Game play

This game is played over the course of a pub crawl. The crawl should consist of nine (or if you're very brave/crazy, 18) different pubs or bars, each representing a golf hole. Before the game, a score-card should be produced which specifies the order of the pubs and which drink should be drunk at each pub. Only one drink is allocated in each pub and this must be the same for every player. In each pub, players get their drinks and the score for that 'hole' is the number of 'sips' it takes for them to finish their drink. (A sip is continuously drinking until you either have to stop or the drink is finished.) This score is noted on that player's score-card.

Penalty points are given for the munching of food during the game, going to the toilet during a hole (using the bog is only permitted before buying your drink at a pub/bar or once it is finished) or for any spillages.

By the end of the pub crawl the person with the lowest score is declared the golf champion. The person with the highest score loses and must suffer a penalty decided beforehand.

This game is often made even more fun if the players dress up in typical golfing attire.

2 arrogance

You need
- A minimum of 4 players
- Alcohol of choice
- A glass
- A coin

The set-up
Sit round a table.

Game play

The first player must pour an amount of alcohol into a glass – the size of the measure depending on how arrogant they are feeling. They must then toss a coin and call heads or tails. If they are correct then the glass is passed to the person to their left, but if they call wrong they have to down the drink. Once the glass has been passed on, the next player must add a chosen amount of their own drink to the same glass (potentially mixing several different types of alcohol) before tossing and calling the coin again.

Variation: Toss the coin twice, the result of the second toss determines whether or not you have to do a dare chosen by the rest of the table.

① touch the cup

Probably the best drinking game ever invented by man.

You need

- A minimum of 3 players
- A pint glass/cup
- A table
- Alcohol of choice
- A coin

The set-up

Sit round the table. At the start of the game, an empty pint glass is filled with a reasonable measure (about a third of a glass) of drink and put in the middle of the table.

Game play

The aim of the game is to take it in turns to bounce the coin off of the table and into the glass. If a player succeeds then they may nominate another player to drink the contents of the glass. If a player bounces the coin and it falls off the table then they themselves must drink the contents. If the player simply misses the glass but the coin stays on the table they pass on the coin without drinking.

Sounds easy? Maybe, but there are four golden rules to remember. If a rule is broken then the penalty is to finish the contents of the cup. The rules are as follows:

① Never touch the cup without first saying (for everybody else to hear) "touch the cup".
② Never put the cup down empty. Always refill it with your own drink first.
③ Never put the cup down without the coin being on the table.
④ Never accept the coin from another player – it must be picked up from the table.

Penalties can stack up and play cannot pass until all penalties have been taken.

Bonus rule: If the coin hits the rim of the glass but does not go in then players around the table have the chance to 'rim challenge' the person who last bounced the coin. If a rim challenge is made then the same player must bounce again. If they miss again then they must finish the contents of the glass. However, if they get it in then the player who challenged them must drink the contents of the glass and then the same amount again.

TOP TIP

Though these games are great for group banter, things can get ugly if you don't know where to draw the line. So have fun but please drink responsibly.

beef and spinach curry

Jesus fed the 5,000 with five loaves of bread and two fish. If only he'd known about our beef and spinach curry! It's a dish of biblical proportions, filling enough to satisfy the most famished of student paupers – no mean feat. We label this as no-nonsense nosh which screams out simplicity and is as cheap as chips. It's great for absorbing the alcohol after that 'quiet drink' at the pub which turned into a marathon session. Or simply a quality, sociable meal for you and your mates to wolf down together. Beef and spinach curry – does exactly what it says on the tin.

beef stewing steak (1kg)

tin of chopped tomatoes (400g)

frozen spinach (400g)

2 large onions

2 cloves of garlic

1 thumb-sized piece of fresh ginger

shot of olive oil

tbsp ground cumin

tsp ground turmeric

tbsp chilli powder

tbsp salt

8 cardamom seeds

naan breads

chop onion, garlic and ginger and fry in oil in large oven-proof saucepan until soft.

cube stewing steak, removing any sinew or gristle.

add to hot pan to sear the meat.

measure out all spices and stir into the pan.

tip in tin of chopped tomatoes and frozen spinach.

bring to boil and stir to break up spinach.

cover with lid.

throw in the oven for 3 hours at 180°C.

remove lid for last half hour and carrying on cooking to get desired consistency.

serve with baked naan breads and ice-cold lager!

serves ❹
£1.80 per portion
20 mins prep ■ 3 hrs cooking

TOP TIP

Do the easy preparation and bung it in the oven. Then wander down the bar for a game of pool and pint or two before heading home to the perfect end to any night – a quality Ruby Murray.

breakfast 'soothie'

Your alarm rings, you hit the snooze button. The second time it goes off you're late for your seminar, which you can't afford to bunk. Again. Whether you're nursing a hangover or recovering from an all-night revision session, you're dying for an easy, quick pick-me-up breakfast.

banana
tbsp honey
small cup of milk
pinch of cinnamon
handful of pecans

peel banana and break into quarters.
throw into blender along with pecans and honey.
season with cinnamon.
blitz till smooth.
add in the milk little by little until you're happy with the consistency and blitz again.
pour into a flask and neck it while sprinting to your lecture.

serves ❶
£0.60 per portion
2 mins prep

DID YOU KNOW?

Milk is great for hangovers as it lines the stomach and soothes any nausea you may be feeling.

sausage and mushroom tortilla

Absinthe. Sambuca. Tequila. Fun at the time, but come the morning after regret sets in and you want to cry 'cos your hangover hurts *that* bad. No sane student wants to cook in this state. Stumble into the kitchen and simply warm up this fry-up alternative, which you cleverly prepared last night. Just whip it out of the fridge, nuke it in the microwave and invite your mates over to laugh at each other's antics from the night before. Banter not victory is what this meal is all about...

8 decent sized sausages

8 eggs

onion

2 medium potatoes

couple of handfuls of mushrooms

2 tins of baked beans

tsp salt

shot of olive oil

WARNING!
Make sure you use an oven-proof pan — these are the ones without plastic handles.

preheat oven to 180°C.

wash, peel and cut potatoes into chunks.

drop into salted water and bring to boil.

simmer for 15 minutes till cooked.

drain.

slice onion and fry together with sausages in oil until golden.

whack in mushrooms and fry for a couple of minutes.

beat eggs in a large bowl and add salt.

grab the potatoes and the other stuff from the pan and stir into the egg mixture.

shove the pan onto the hob and make sure it's smoking hot before spilling in the egg contents.

launch immediately into the oven for 20-25 minutes. Once set and golden on top, take out.

allow to cool in pan for 5-10 minutes.

loosen around the edges and turn out.
Happy times…

serves **6**
£1.20 per portion
5 mins prep ■ 35 mins cooking

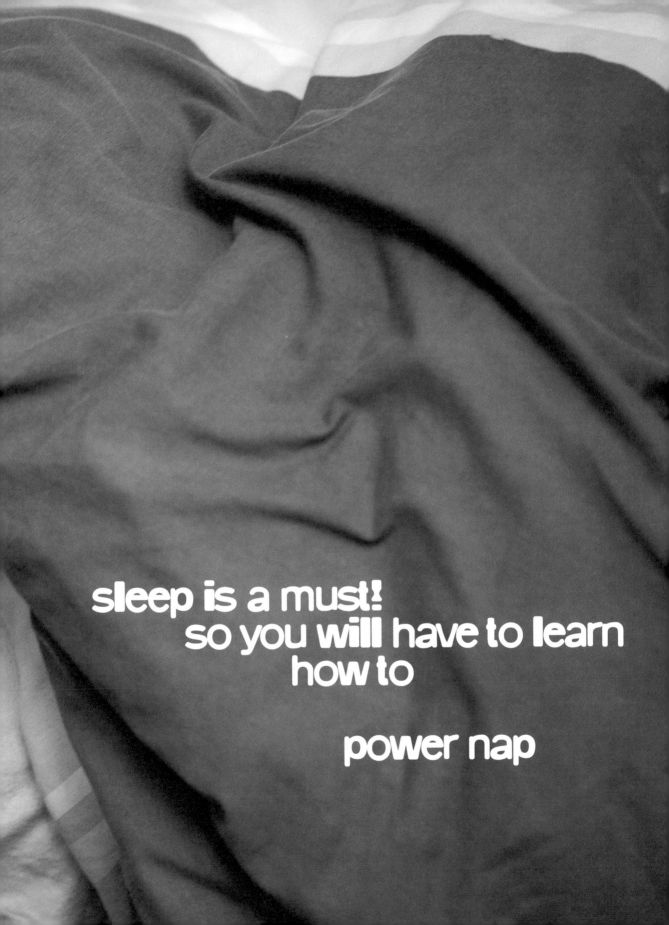

sleep is a must!
so you will have to learn
how to

power nap

banana bread

We've never met a wimpy gorilla, and we put this ape's awesome athleticism partly down to eating the humble banana. This is because bananas are extremely nutritious; rich in potassium, riboflavin, niacin and fibre, and the rapid energy boost given by their high sugar levels means that they're a great snack. We've invented a nifty way to get one of your five portions of fruit a day through simply making and eating your own bread.

plain flour (300g)
1 ½ tsp baking powder
pinch of salt
castor sugar (50g)
butter (50g)
2 eggs
2 ripe bananas
handful of walnuts (50g)

preheat oven to 180°C.
sieve dry ingredients together and stir in sugar.
melt butter and beat the eggs.
mash bananas and add to dry ingredients with butter and beaten eggs.
beat well to mix evenly. Stir through walnuts.
slop mixture into a loaf tin and bake for an hour.
turn out of tin to cool.

serves ❽
£0.40 per portion
10 mins prep ■ 1 hr cooking

cherry and almond muffins

Do you enjoy popping cherries and toasting nuts? If the answer is yes then look no further than our muffin to end all muffins. This ingenious mishmash of soft juicy cherries with mixed nuts hidden here and there is enough to shut up any grumbling stomach in between lectures. Even better, rub it in your mate's face while you scoff down this treasure and watch as they fork out for the extortionate coffee shop substitute.

tin of stoned cherries (400g)
milk (300ml)
butter (80g)
large egg
plain flour (350g)
caster sugar (200g)
flaked almonds (80g)
2 tsp baking powder
pinch of salt
pinch of cinnamon

preheat oven to 180°C.

sieve dry ingredients together in a bowl.

melt butter in microwave and beat in the egg.

combine wet and dry ingredients and stir to bring together.

add drained cherries and mix, taking care not to break them up too much.

lay out 12 paper muffin cases on a baking tray and dollop a heaped tbsp of mix into each.

sprinkle with demerara sugar and bake for 20 minutes until risen and starting to crack.

enjoy fresh, straight from the oven or even better as amid-morning snack the day after.

makes ⑫
£0.25 per portion
10 mins prep ■ 20 mins baking

tips and tricks

"Neck it, fresher." "See it off." "Down it!" These phrases make up the basic vocabulary of the student. So to avoid embarrassment when you have to consume your drink in one, we recommend choosing your drink carefully. Always go for flat, sweet drinks. They'll travel down your gullet at breakneck speed.

Fancy dress. Halloween masks, Christmas tinsel, that monkey costume you wore for charity... remember to bring any whacky gear with you from home as your fresher's parties will require you to dress like an idiot on a regular basis. You'll outshine those budget outfits and look like a fancy dress expert.

Nightclub bouncers are always wrong. BUT when you're with them they are always RIGHT! Don't ever argue with them, they WILL chuck you out.

Know your cash machines. When you're drunk it can seem worth the £1.50 to withdraw from an ATM which charges, but those precious pounds quickly build up over the course of a year. Find the non-charging ones early and don't forget 'em.

Keep a bottle opener on your key ring. Helps you out in those potentially molar-breaking situations and is a class conversation starter at house parties.

You may be drunk but don't mess with fire extinguishers. We at **SORTED** have had our fair share of beastings followed by hefty fines 'cos we thought using safety equipment as a super soaker was funny. Some universities might even chuck you off your course. Live and learn, guys...

Think of your stomach
The news students all around the UK have been waiting for: the greasy fry-up may actually be good for you! The morning after a killer night out drinking, a fry-up is great for providing the energy you need. Fat contains lots of calories; eggs and meat are rich in protein; and the breakfast is also salty which is another bonus for your addled mind and body.

Marmite on toast helps replace lost vitamin B. It works. Love it or hate it. Actually, food is a good idea all round – before, during and immediately after drinking. Food doesn't absorb alcohol, but it does increase metabolism, activates alcohol absorption, and increases the speed with which the body processes alcohol.

Doctor's jargon
Alcohol acts as a diuretic. In case those long hours spent at the urinal didn't tip you off, more is going out than coming in. You need to replace that liquid. To solve this problem **SORTED** has come up with a nifty idea – *The Bottle Cap Trick*. Every time you crack open another can/bottle save the ring-pull or cap. Before you hit the sack count your drink receipts and down 100ml of water for every guilty cap or ring-pull.
For example:
six cans of lager = six ring pulls = 600ml (just over a pint) of water.

RECIPES

* blueberry flapjack

* scrambled eggs with smoked mackerel

* thai-style tuna burgers

* brainy sandwich filler

* squash snd sage soup

* grilled fish salad

* crunchy, creamy chicken satay

* simple sushi

brain boosters

The Four Horsemen of the Apocalypse gallop around the exam room, flashing rude gestures at you while chanting "class retard!" As you look down at your exam paper, sweating and losing focus, it's gutting to admit that their mockery is justified. This is your one opportunity and you choke. While you were out getting lashed the past couple of nights, your mates had been secretly revising and now you're gonna look like a grade A moron. Exam time – they might as well rename it doomsday. If only you had done it differently...

Let's rewind. Here's where we come in. Food is the fuel for your brain and body. Treat your body like a temple and you'll reap the rewards. In this section we'll be parading the nosh that will knock up those IQ points which drink has cruelly taken away. So buck up and take a deep breath as we feed you some tasty, brainy recipes fit for a rocket scientist. Not only will these dishes boost your grades, but they'll also save you from having to make that embarrassing call to your parents explaining how you flunked...

And remember, keep an eye on our website at www.sortedfood.com for more great recipes.

blueberry flapjack

This blueberry flapjack (a bargain bucket item for less than 40p a slice) will keep for days and is considered by us a gold-dust commodity during exam time. However, a word of advice: lock them in the safety of your room otherwise your mates will snap 'em up once they know they're in your food cupboard!

rolled oats or porridge oats (300g)
fresh blueberries (150g)
golden syrup (200g)
butter (170g)
4 tbsp brown sugar
tsp ground cinnamon

preheat oven to 180°C.
melt butter, sugar, syrup and cinnamon in a saucepan.
bubble for a minute before removing from heat.
fold in oats until fully combined.
scatter blueberries into mix and carefully stir through.
tip mix into deep baking tray.
bake for 20-25 minutes until golden.
cool in tin, cutting into portions before completely cold.

makes ⑫
£0.40 per portion
5 mins prep ■ 25 mins cooking

NOTE

Uni work = depressing. The cooked oats will zap any fatigue bothering you, allowing you to be on the ball for those lengthy revisions sessions.

DID YOU KNOW?

A recent study involving rats has shown blueberries to be helpful in slowing down or stopping memory loss and improving short-term memory. Yeah right, like rats have a lot to recall, try being a student.

scrambled eggs with smoked mackerel

Eggs and fish? That's right. Eggs AND fish. If you're gagging at the thought of this 'chuck-up-your-guts' combo, give us a chance to explain. The essential fatty oils of the mackerel combined with the protein from the eggs, all spread on a slab of carb-heavy bread, is the secret to keeping that vital organ in between your ears active. And it don't taste half bad either! The brain food fave of Einstein (don't ask us to prove that), it'll give you the edge you need the morning before an exam. Just make sure you've done some revision as well though, yeah?

2 large eggs
smoked mackerel fillet (100g)
chunky granary bread
splash of milk
knob of butter
chopped parsley

crack eggs into bowl, add milk and whisk.

melt butter in a pan over gentle heat.

chop parsley finely.

skin mackerel fillets and flake into pieces.

throw egg and milk mix and fish into pan and stir continuously.

toast bread till golden.

stir eggs till the mixture thickens and mix in parsley.

add pinch of salt and pepper to season.

dollop scrambled egg onto toast and serve with orange juice or a steaming cup of tea.

serves ❶
£1.60 per portion
2 mins prep ■ 5 mins cooking

thai-style tuna burgers

This cheap and easy burger will help boost the IQ points lost during lengthy procrastination sessions in the dreaded exam period. A light and healthy meal which is high in omega-3 oils (fresh tuna is chocka with these, but tinned is cheaper), it'll taste like it's from the greasy spoon café but without the guilt trip. Quality nosh for sharing with your study buddy. Go on, you've earned it.

small tin of tuna in brine

2 pitta breads

egg

lime

tsp chopped chilli

clump of fresh coriander

tsp fresh ginger

fistful of mixed salad leaves

mayonnaise

sweet chilli sauce

dusting of flour

shot of olive oil

squeeze out as much brine as possible from tinned tuna and place into bowl.

zest the lime into the bowl with finely chopped chilli, ginger and coriander.

crack in the egg and mix it up.

pack and shape into 4 burgers.

dust with flour and fry in oil in pan till crisp, golden and hot right through.

warm the pitta breads in a toaster, cut into halves and open pockets.

spread on mayonnaise, chuck in salad leaves, slot in a burger and top it off with chilli sauce to dip.

stuff your face and enjoy.

serves ❷
£0.80 per portion
5 mins prep ■ 5 mins cooking

help yourself to stay alert, sharp and ready

for action

brainy sandwich filler

The **SORTED** team prays daily to the Subway gods who create their lush sarnies. However, such luxuries come at a cost. So, rather than blow your loan daily on the 'sub of the day', save a mint and make a delicious alternative that you can pack to take with you on the go. Your mates may rib you for a while, but once they're skint and begging you to buy the next round, you'll have their proverbial nuts in the palm of your hand.

ripe avocado
¼ red onion
granary bread
fistful of watercress
dash of balsamic vinegar
cluster of pine nuts
pinch of salt

toast pine nuts in a hot dry pan.
scoop flesh from avocado and slice.
wash watercress.
combine all ingredients with thinly sliced red onion.
smear between two doorstep slices of bread and tuck in.

serves ❶
£1.20 per portion
5 mins prep ■ 1 min cooking

squash and sage soup

Whether you have that essay due in last minute or need to leg it to the library to avoid a hefty fine, this is the ideal stress reliever. The therapeutic sage pauses the world around you, allowing you time to think.

large butternut squash
large onion
double cream (200ml)
shot of olive oil
knob of butter
tbsp honey
few fresh sage leaves
vegetable stock cube
litre of water

preheat oven to 200°C.

peel, deseed and chop the squash into thumb-sized pieces.

toss in olive oil, a pinch of salt and roast for half an hour until squash begins to soften.

dice onion roughly and sweat off in a lidded pan with butter until clear.

drizzle in honey and heat till it bubbles.

crumble in stock cube and add water, squash and torn sage.

simmer for 20 minutes.

blitz to a smooth soup.

finish with cream and seasoning, and serve in bowl or slurp straight from a mug.

serves **6**
£0.80 per portion
5 mins prep ■ 1 hr cooking

> ### DID YOU KNOW?
> The herb sage is associated with improved memory, especially the memory of dreams. You never know, this green herb of the Earth may turn you into a super geek and make you dream about what you've revised. The ultimate lazy revision schedule.

grilled fish salad

To students the word 'exams' brings about the same imminent fear as phrases such as, "you have insufficient funds for withdrawal" or "sorry mate, that's last orders". However, there's good news... we have invented a superhero snacky lunch with brain-awakening qualities that'll have you flying through those test papers. The combination of oily fish, egg, leafy greens and potatoes helps to fuel the brain, that demanding organ which uses up 30 per cent of the body's daily calories and nutrients. Keep it pumped up and ready for action.

2 trout fillets

4 new potatoes

egg

tomato

fistful of spinach and watercress salad

half a dozen black pitted olives

wedge of lemon

french vinaigrette

boil potatoes in pan of salted water for 8 minutes.
drop egg into same pan for a further 6 minutes.
cool both potato and egg under cold running water.
quarter tomato, potato, olives and peeled egg.
dress salad leaves, potatoes and olives in vinaigrette.
arrange eggs and tomatoes on a plate.
grill seasoned trout fillets for 2-3 minutes.
lay the fillets on the salad bed.
squeeze the lemon over fish.

serves ❶
£2.60 per portion
15 mins prep ■ 4 mins cooking

get comfortable, enjoy your work.
pace yourself and
don't let it

control you

crunchy, creamy chicken satay

Summer term at uni is a mixture of heaven and hell. Hell begins when your exams start but paradise beckons once they're over. So what better way to celebrate the end of your brain-slogging sessions and officially kick off the barbecue season than with these fancy little satay sticks. Chuck these on the barbie, rustle up the sauce and serve with salad or rice. Chill out in the sun – whilst planning your summer holiday...

4 chicken breasts

2 mugs of rice

⅓ jar of balti curry paste

large onion

3 cloves of garlic

tin of coconut milk (400g)

jar of crunchy peanut butter (250g)

shot of cooking oil

handful of fresh coriander

cube chicken into 1 in chunks and rub with oil and curry paste, leaving to marinate for a while.

slice onion and crush the garlic. Fry in saucepan until soft and sweet.

thread chicken pieces onto 8 skewers (pre-soaked in water for 30 mins) and stack on a plate.

scoop peanut butter out of jar, add to the onions with coconut milk and the remainder of the marinade.

boil rice in a large pan of salted water as per packet instructions until light and fluffy.

grill skewers under a hot grill or on the BBQ, turning occasionally.

drain rice and pile onto a plate, top with skewers and ladle over sauce.

sprinkle with freshly chopped coriander.

serves ❹
£2.40 per portion
10 mins prep ■ 20 mins cooking

simple sushi

It's a cruel world being a student. When the locals at your university pub jeer at you for being a tax-evading leech on society it can be a blow to your ego. It's at times like these when you need to convince yourself that you're multicultural and worldly-wise again. This dish ticks all the boxes.

sushi rice (250g)

6 nori sheets (seaweed sheets)

handful of cooked prawns

6 seafood sticks

handful of smoked salmon offcuts

avocado

bunch of spring onions

knob of fresh or pickled ginger

½ cucumber

tbsp caster sugar

tbsp rice wine vinegar

tbsp mirin (japanese rice wine)

¼ tube wasabi paste

tsp salt

soy sauce to dip

wash rice under cold running water and cook according to packet instructions, adding salt, sugar, vinegar and mirin when boiled.

transfer cooked rice to a bowl and allow to cool.

prepare all the fillings by cutting into thin strips.

lay out a nori seaweed sheet on the work surface (or sushi mat if available) and flick a small amount of water onto it.

spread cooled rice over the sheet to a thickness of 1cm. Leave a small margin at the sides.

brush a little wasabi paste over the rice. Take care – it's hot stuff! If in doubt taste a little first.

arrange your fillings in a line. Ensure all ingredients appear all the way along the sheet because it will be cut.

roll the sheet up tightly and dampen the end to stick it down.

wrap in clingfilm and store in fridge until required.

slice into 3cm pieces with damp knife and serve with chopsticks and soy sauce to dip.

serves ❹

£1.40 per portion

20 mins prep ■ 20 mins cooking

tips and tricks

You might have been 'Clever Trevor' in school. At uni there's gonna be a bunch of students smarter than you. So, make as many mates on your course as early as you can; you'll soon notice the benefits, especially when you get stuck on that 5,000 word essay...

Library fines. If not treated with respect these can mount up and murder your week's budget. Keep updated on your book loans and, more importantly, get to know the library team – it could ultimately be the difference between a night out and a night in.

Books. Save yourself a pretty penny and borrow the core textbooks you need for your course from the library. Be quick though as there'll be other students thinking the same thing! If all else fails go online to Amazon or eBay, or even have a gander at second-hand student book fairs at your union – anything to avoid shelling out the full retail price!

Teaching staff. Whatever you've been told, lecturers aren't that clued up on who they teach. However, your seminar tutors will be and they are the real teaching gods who will answer all your annoying questions. Get to know them.

Think ahead. Make sure you visit PC World and max out on one of those fancy printer/scanner/photocopier combos. It'll save you a ton of cash on printing credits and you won't have the hassle of facing that 11.59pm dash to the library to print off your midnight deadline essay.

Green tea. It isn't just for hippies. Recent research shows that the non-caffeinated tea is soothing for the nerves and can relieve stress by making the thinking process cleaner and more logical. So the

Life after uni
The last thing on your mind when you get to uni is your career, but if you pull your finger out and do a little research it can go a long way. Placements, internships and charity projects abroad during the summer will sex up your CV and make you look 'well rounded'. Make the most of these opportunities and you might be sorted for a job in the scary real world once you finish.

occasional cup might just help you from freaking out before that big exam.

Sports drinks. They may provide that quick energy boost you're after but the rush won't last and can even lead to a noticeable decline in energy later in the day. Drinking plain old water for maximum hydration may be your best bet.

Laptops. Bring one. It'll save you the hassle of dragging all your books and folders to the library whenever you need to do work. Halls often have super-fast broadband which allows you to download at sonic speed.

Get
Sorted.

RECIPES

MEAL 1

* spicy red pepper soup

* lamb with ratatouille

* cheeky chocolate cherry pots

MEAL 2

* warm asparagus and beetroot salad

* chilli garlic prawns on a lemon saffron risotto

* sublime strawberry 'champagne' jelly

MEAL 3

* red onion tartlet with creamy goats cheese

* gorgonzola gnocchi with spinach and
    toasted walnuts

* baileys soufflé-style ice cream

        morning after... eggs benedict

meals to impress

Finding yourself a boyfriend or girlfriend at uni doesn't come cheap and eating out together can also eat away at your loan. During the sickeningly cringey 'honeymoon' period money slips out of your fingers and you even start tossing over golden shrapnel to the local tramps. Before you know it, the floating halo above your other half's head disappears and reality hits you where it hurts. All that wining and dining, supposed one-off treats and silly childish gifts mount up, and your bank manager is having a right fit. You need to somehow bring the spark back into your relationship without filing for bankruptcy. And no, selling your body on the streets isn't an option.

We proudly present you with the solution – delicious and dead easy dishes that will soon have you right back in the apple of your eye's good books. Picture the scene: you're enjoying a classy three-course monster while surrounded by a blaze of scented candles and listening to Barry White. Alternatively, if you're a hard up student: you're eating a posh (but cheap) meal in the pitch black (apart from the flickering desk lamp you've left on in an attempt to create a 'sexy' atmosphere) while trying to drown out your noisy mates in the kitchen who are playing drinking games. Who said romance was dead?

And remember, keep an eye on our website at www.sortedfood.com for more great recipes.

spicy red pepper soup

One for the cold winter months. What you need during this time is comfort food that will melt your hot date into submission – this meal's the key to securing that all-important clincher. We've designed a three-course extravaganza that will knock the socks off any student bum. Allow us to introduce our opening act of spicy wholesome soup, followed by a headliner of posh meat and two veg, succeeded by a firework finale we call cheeky chocolate cherry pots.

shot of olive oil
large onion
3 red peppers
large potato
½ tsp paprika
¼ tsp chilli powder
vegetable stock cube
fistful of freshly chopped chives
dollop of natural yoghurt

DID YOU KNOW?

The active ingredient in hot red peppers is a compound called capsaicin, which gives it that unique sting. Capsaicin triggers the release of endorphins in the brain, which has a pain-relieving effect similar to that of morphine.

slice onion and fry in oil in deep pan for 5-10 minutes.
de-seed and roughly chop the peppers, peel and grate the potato and then add both to the cooked onions.
pour in 750ml (a pint and a bit) of water and sprinkle in stock cube and spices.
simmer for half an hour.
blitz to a smooth soup, return to pan, reheat and season.
whisk in the yoghurt, having removed the pan from the heat, and stir through the chopped chives. Serve.
tear off some crusty rustic bread to dunk in this warming soup.

serves ❹
£1.20 per portion
10 mins prep ■ 45 mins cooking

WARNING!

Chilli powder can be the work of the devil in the wrong hands. A powerful spice, it can ruin a romantic night if meandering mitts meet sensitive parts of the body. Don't be a mug — remember to wash your hands.

lamb with ratatouille

lamb neck fillet (600g)
8 medium tomatoes
2 red peppers
red onion
aubergine
3 courgettes
2 cloves of garlic

6 wholemeal pitta breads
sprinkle of fresh mint
handful of feta cheese
tbsp fennel seeds
2 shots of olive oil
2 tbsp flour

dice tomatoes, onion, peppers, aubergine and courgettes into 1in cubes to make your raw ratatouille. Crush the garlic.

transfer to a large baking tray.

drizzle over olive oil, season generously with salt and black pepper.

roast at 200°C for 40 minutes, tossing occasionally.

mix fennel seeds and flour together on a board.

roll the lamb over the flour/fennel seed mix until you achieve an even coating.

fry the lamb, just before the ratatouille is ready, in a pan until golden on all sides. Slide it into the same oven for 5 minutes (rare), 8 minutes (medium) or 12 minutes (well done).

rest the meat for couple of minutes before slicing.

stir mint through the ratatouille.

slip pitta breads into a toaster till crisp.

slice into strips.

spoon ratatouille onto a plate and crumble over feta cheese.

lay the lamb on top with pitta on the side.

serves **4**
£3.00 per portion
15 mins prep ■ 45 mins cooking

meal
1

Chocolate contains methylxanthines. As technical as these sound and as tricky as they are to say they work wonders, stimulating conduction and transmission of nerve impulses, helping to heighten sensitivity.

cheeky chocolate cherry pots

butter (100g)

plain chocolate (100g)

large egg

brown sugar (100g)

4 tbsp self-raising flour

4 tbsp pitted morello cherries (in syrup)

cream

preheat oven to 220°C.

grease 4 ramekins with butter and drop a layer of drained cherries into the base of each.

snap chocolate into cubes and place with diced butter into a plastic bowl.

melt butter and chocolate over a pan of simmering water or, even easier, in the microwave.

whisk egg and sugar in another bowl until light and fluffy (about 2 minutes).

pour in the melted chocolate mix and beat again to combine.

sieve in the flour and fold carefully until smooth.

share between the ramekins, then bake for 20-25 minutes until risen and just cracking on top.

invert puddings onto a plate and carefully shake them out.

drizzle with cream and serve.

serves **4**
£0.60 per portion
10 mins prep ■ 25 mins cooking

NOTE
Although spongy on the outside the puds should still be gooey in the centre. Very rich and dangerously sensuous.

warm asparagus and beetroot salad

When you have someone special round to your place the last thing you want to do is bloat the hell out of 'em by stuffing them with enough food to feed a baby elephant. Consequently, a bout of flatulence and tiredness follows, which ain't good for anyone. This summery three-course menu is as light as a Quaver, with a hassle-free starter, a tangy twisty risotto for main and a sublime jelly to finish. This menu is so sexy, seductive and cool we guarantee your partner'll be putty in your hands by the final mouthful.

bunch of asparagus spears
small pack of cooked salad beetroot
dash of white wine vinegar
dollop of horseradish sauce
fistful of fresh parsley
scattering of parmesan shavings
2 shots of olive oil
couple of spring onions

meal
2

trim the stalky base from asparagus spears and wash.

place on baking tray, toss in a shot of oil and season with salt and pepper.

roast at 200°C for about 6-8 minutes until slightly soft to touch.

chop beetroot into bite-sized pieces and add to the almost cooked asparagus to heat through.

whisk remaining oil, horseradish sauce and vinegar together to create dressing. Season.

arrange asparagus and beetroot on a plate so they overlap.

sprinkle over Parmesan shavings, garnish with parsley and finely sliced spring onioins, then drizzle with dressing.

enjoy as a perfectly delicate start to any romantic meal.

serves ❷
£1.20 per portion
5 mins prep ■ 12 mins cooking

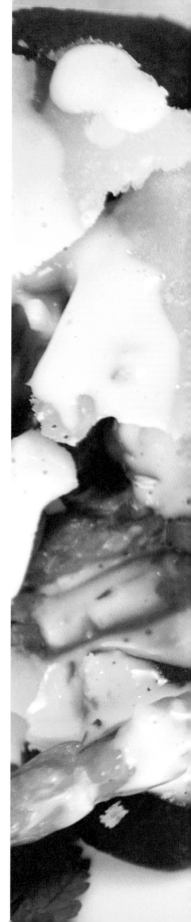

Asparagus contains vitamin A, phosphorus and boosts androsterone levels, which is an odourless hormone released by men. This, along with their suggestive shape, can really heat up any sensuous situation.

chilli garlic prawns on a lemon saffron risotto

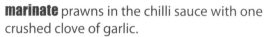

raw prawns (250g)

risotto rice (250g)

lemon

4 tbsp sweet chilli sauce

3 cloves of garlic

tsp grated fresh ginger

knob of butter

litre of water

vegetable stock cube

pinch of saffron

bunch of spring onions

fistful of fresh parsley

drizzle of double cream

marinate prawns in the chilli sauce with one crushed clove of garlic.

dissolve stock cube in water and infuse saffron in the stock by bringing it to a simmer.

slice spring onions and chop the ginger and remaining garlic.

sweat onions, ginger and garlic in a deep pan with the butter for a few moments.

stir in the rice to coat all the grains in butter.

zest in the lemon and add a ladle of stock at a time, stirring continuously.

add more stock as the previous ladle is absorbed. Should take about 20 minutes.

heat a dry frying pan when the rice is plump and cooked.

toss in the prawns and marinade and sizzle until prawns turn pink all over.

drizzle cream into risotto and finish with chopped parsley and lemon juice.

season.

spoon risotto onto plates and top with prawns.

serves ❷
£2.80 per portion
5 mins prep ■ 25 mins cooking

meal 2

sublime strawberry 'champagne' jelly

½ bottle rosé cava (375ml)
caster sugar (175g)
gelatin (10g of powder or 4 leaves)
handful of fresh strawberries
few sprigs of fresh mint

pop the cava's cork and glug a quarter of the bottle into a pan.

spoon in the sugar and bring to the boil; simmer until sugar has dissolved.

soak gelatin (if using leaves) in cold water, squeeze dry and whisk into the hot 'champagne'.

cool the mixture by sitting pan in cold water.

trickle another quarter of the bottle of cava into the gelatin mix, trying to maintain as much fizz as possible.

stir through very finely shredded mint leaves.

share the mixture between 2 glasses.

submerge sliced strawberries in the jelly and leave in the fridge to set.

enjoy with whipped cream for really posh jelly dessert!

serves ❷
£1.60 per portion
5 mins prep ■ 60 mins to set

NOTE

If you have time you can layer the jelly by filling the glasses up only a third at a time and setting in the fridge. Each time the fruit will remain in suspension rather than floating to the top. The jelly you're not setting will remain liquid if kept in a warm room for long enough.

meal
2

red onion tartlet with creamy goats cheese

As the song goes, "those were the best days of my life, back in the summer of '69". Though the summer may be over and with the new academic year looming in September, we suggest you and your 'special' friend ignore the dark horizon and turn your attention instead to this hidden gem. A delicately balanced onion and goats cheese tartlet teases your palette before a plate of feisty Italian dumplings obliterates that insatiable student appetite, all topped off with a stupefyingly tasty Baileys soufflé-style ice cream. Temptation, fulfilment, pleasure...

sheet of ready-rolled puff pastry (125g)

goats cheese (75g)

red onion

bundle of fresh basil leaves

couple of pitted black olives

few cherry tomatoes

handful of crisp salad leaves

drizzle of salad dressing

tbsp brown sugar

tbsp balsamic vinegar

shot of olive oil

preheat oven to 200°C.

peel and slice onion as thinly as possible.

fry in oil for 10 minutes until soft and sweet.

splash in vinegar and sugar and heat for 5 minutes until onions are sticky and marmalade-like.

roll out pastry and cut out two rectangles about the size of your hand.

place these on a baking tray and score a 1cm margin around the edge.

prick the inner section of each rectangle all over with a fork and bake in oven for 10 minutes until puffed up and golden.

cut into that scored mark again and discard the centre section. It should resemble a vol-au-vent with a lip around the edge, forming a well in the centre.

spoon in some onion marmalade, crumble over goats cheese, quartered cherry tomatoes and torn basil leaves.

return to oven for 5 minutes to melt cheese and serve on a bed of dressed salad with halved olives.

serves ❷
£1.20 per portion
15 mins prep ■ 25 mins cooking

Basil increases blood circulation, enhances sex drive and increases fertility. Basil oil was once used as a perfume by Mediterranean prostitutes to attract customers. Perhaps not quite what you're looking for but why knock it if it works for you and your partner.

meal 3

gorgonzola gnocchi with spinach and toasted walnuts

potato gnocchi (250g–shop bought)

creamy gorgonzola cheese (50g)

2 large fistfuls of fresh spinach

knob of butter

double cream (50ml)

cluster of walnuts

fresh parmesan

fill a pan with salted water and bring to the boil.

wash spinach under cold running water and drain well.

drop gnocchi into boiling water and cook for 4 minutes until they float.

wilt spinach in a hot pan with the butter before adding cream and walnuts.

crumble over Gorgonzola and season with freshly ground black pepper.

drain gnocchi and toss in the creamy spinach sauce.

divide between bowls and grate Parmesan over to serve.

serves ❷
£1.40 per portion
2 mins prep ■ 5 mins cooking

meal
3

baileys soufflé-style ice cream

egg white (75ml – about 2 eggs' worth)
caster sugar (75g)
double cream (150ml)
handful of toasted almonds
baileys to taste (about a double shot)

whip the egg white until it holds in soft peaks when the whisk is removed and beat in the caster sugar.

whisk up the cream to the same stage in another bowl.

toast almonds in a dry pan until golden.

fold the cream and egg whites together.

lace with the Baileys (as much as you like – about 50ml is right) and stir through the almonds so everything is well-combined.

spoon into small teacups, ramekins or similar moulds.

cover with clingfilm and freeze overnight.

dip in hot water to loosen edges and turn out to serve.

garnish with fresh berries and more toasted almonds.

serves ❷
£0.80 per portion
10 mins prep ■ overnight freezing

NOTE

Technically this is not actually a soufflé, as it contains no egg yolk. But the light, airy consistency resembles one — they'll never know.

meal
3

morning after...
eggs benedict

"Who's Benedict?" we hear you ask. There are differing accounts as to the origin of this dish, but we think his full name was Lemuel Benedict, an American city slicker who in 1894 walked into New York's Waldorf Hotel with a killer hangover and asked for "buttered toast, poached eggs, crisp bacon and a hooker of hollandaise". The maitre d' was so impressed with the idea that he put Benedict's dish on the menu and, alas, this simple dish was born. It's the ideal breakfast for impressing your other half and making them think you're one hell of a catch. Stuff it down their neck fast before they realise it's only an idiot-proof fry-up...

2 large eggs

2 chunky slices of granary bread

4 hefty slices of good quality ham

packet of hollandaise sauce powder (30g)

milk (300ml)

bring pan of salted water to the boil.

heat milk in a separate pan and whisk in the hollandaise powder until smooth.

bring to simmer, stirring as it thickens.

stir the salted water quickly in the pan to create a spiral effect and crack an egg into the centre of the well. Allow to poach for 3-4 minutes.

remove and keep warm while repeating with other egg.

toast slices of granary bread, butter them and drape the ham over each slice.

position a softly poached egg on top of the ham and spoon the hollandaise over one side.

serve immediately and break into the yolk to watch it ooze.

serves ❷
£0.80 per portion
10 mins cooking

RECIPES

* swiss-style muesli

* jacket potato with tuna sorrento

* vegetable pesto couscous

* californian ranch & hoisin crab wraps

* apricot and ginger gratin

* chunky chocolate brownies

* lemon and blackcurrant fool

odds & sods

In 1972, a plane carrying a Uruguayan rugby team crashed into the snow-covered Argentine Andes mountains. With barely any food and no hope of immediate rescue, you might say the team were in a sticky situation. Unfortunately for them, Domino's Pizza didn't deliver to that region. What a bummer. So what did they do? They ate each other. That's right. When you're backed into a corner, you have to make some tough calls.

At some point during your uni career you too may be faced with a similarly harrowing decision. Do you smear on some BBQ sauce and take a bite out of the guy in your class who always asks annoying questions? Well hopefully you won't have to because we've created some nimble dishes that you can chuck together when you're down to your last penny but need a little something for that special occasion. This chapter is your last-minute get-out clause for any tight situation. Random, useful and bordering on genius…

And remember, keep an eye on our website at www.sortedfood.com for more great recipes.

university is one long ride,
so enjoy the journey...

swiss-style muesli

Okay, it's not the most appealing looking cereal but wait until you taste our recipe! This muesli ticks all the boxes: it's quick, full of vitamins and is a long-lasting energy food that'll fill the biggest stomach. Stash it under your bed and it's always there when you forget to stock up on usual supplies. Try it with apple juice rather than milk.

4 mugs of porridge oats
sultanas (120g)
dried apricots (120g)
chopped hazelnuts (120g)
coconut shavings (80g)
splash of apple juice
natural yoghurt
honey or maple syrup
cinnamon

mix the dried ingredients together and stash in airtight container until you need it.

place as much as you want into a bowl and splash over the apple juice about half way up the bowl.

dollop some natural yoghurt on top.

drizzle with honey or maple syrup and/or sprinkle with cinnamon.

serves **6**
£0.50 per portion
2 mins prep

NOTE
The dried fruit and nuts can be swapped/substituted for similar quantities of:

Dried apple
Dried cranberries
Dried mango
Banana chips

Almonds
Walnuts
Coconut shavings
Sunflower seeds
Pumpkin seeds

jacket potato with tuna sorrento

The Irish love spuds and so do we. Why? 'Cos we're trampy students and potatoes are cheap. When you become a full-time student you'll understand the novelty of 'scumming it' now and again (wearing the same underwear for days on end, living in a freezing house 'cos someone forgot to pay the gas bill, and so on). So when you're stuck in this depressing state, remember the humble jacket potato because it'll stick by you through thick and thin. All it needs is a nuke in the microwave, finished in the oven and stuffed with a top-grade filling of either ratatouille (see page 128 – lamb with ratatouille), bacon and brie, BBQ baked beans or the little tuna mayo adaptation you see here.

2 large jacket potatoes
2 x 185g tins of tuna
tin of red kidney beans
bunch of spring onions
dollop of mayonnaise
shot of olive oil

prick potatoes with a fork and rub with oil.

bake at 180°C for about 1½-2 hours depending on their size.

drain tuna and kidney beans and put in bowl.

chop the spring onions and add to the tuna along with the mayonnaise.

season with salt (be careful – if the tuna was in brine it may not need salt) and pepper and mix well.

slash open the potato and load on the filling.

serves ❷
£1.20 per portion
5 mins prep ■ 90 mins cooking

NOTE
To save time chuck the potatoes in the microwave on full power for 8–10 minutes before finishing them in the oven for 10 minutes to crisp up the skin. Test to see if they're cooked by pushing a knife into the middle. It should slide in like, erm, a knife through butter and the blade should come out hot.

make the most of what you've got!

mugs make perfect bowls!

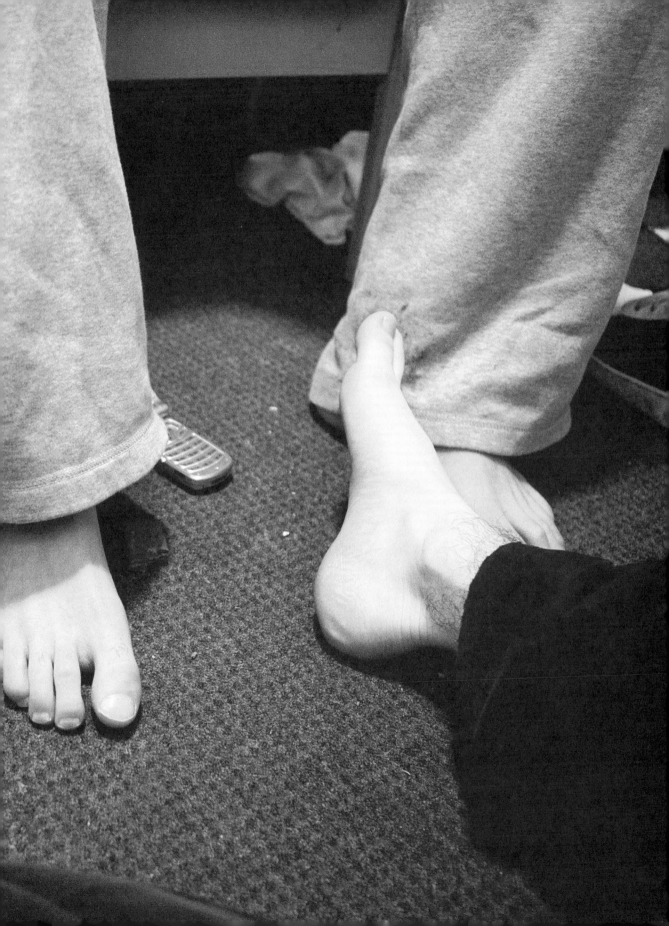

on the go

At uni, even the big boys get homesick. At some point, once your liver is spent, you too might fancy going home for the weekend. If so, prepare for that long, boring train journey ahead and make these tasty wraps and salads to avoid getting shafted by the inflated buffet cart prices. Those extra pennies in your pocket will have you laughing all the way down to the pub. Salads – a quid; wraps – couple of pounds; the look on other passengers' faces once they see how good your lunch is – priceless.

vegetable pesto couscous

You're at the uni gym for the first time in donkey's years and you go for *that* pre-session weigh in. Weeks of relentless drinking and binged-up kebab sessions have cost you and you're now as heavy as Homer Simpson. Alarm bells ring and you panic as you try to mentally organise a healthy eating plan. Well, for a start, look no further than this veggie pesto couscous – an ideal way to begin a detox. Light, full of flavour and, best of all, low in calories, it's tasty enough to fill you up without having to fight your conscience. Effortless healthy eating...

couscous (200g)
vegetable stock cube
small jar of green pesto
red pepper
yellow pepper

aubergine
courgette
red onion
3 cloves of garlic
2 shots of olive oil

hack up all the vegetables into irregular shaped mouth-sized pieces and throw into a deep baking tray.

toss in olive oil and crush over the garlic.

roast in a very hot oven for 15 minutes.

boil the kettle and pour 250ml water over the crumbled stock cube in a bowl.

dump the couscous into this boiling stock, cover with a plate and leave to absorb for 5 minutes.

fluff up the couscous with a fork and tip in the roasted vegetables and pesto.

stir, season and allow to cool completely.

store in tupperware for the perfect picnic in the park, travel snack or post-gym boost.

serves ❹
£1.20 per portion
10 mins prep ■ 15 mins cooking

californian ranch & hoisin crab wraps

If mums made packed lunches *this* good, school dinner ladies would be out of a job. So scrimp on your pennies and take our advice with this ultimate uni packed-lunch wrap. With an irresistible mix of avocado, ripe tomato and ham spread on a bed of cream cheese and wrapped in a soft tortilla, the Californian ranch wraps will have you dribbling for more. For an oriental twist, try the crab drizzled in hoisin sauce – your mates will think you're a chef *par excellence*. Make this first thing in the morning and take as lunch. Be warned though, they're so good you'll need sheer willpower to stop yourself scoffing 'em there and then.

californian ranch wraps

4 x 10in flour tortillas

2 ripe avocados

4 ripe tomatoes

small tub of garlic and herb cream cheese

pack of pre-cooked sliced turkey or chicken

spread the cream cheese over one side of each tortilla, going right to the edges.

halve the avocados, remove stones and scoop out flesh. Slice lengthways.

drape the cooked turkey or chicken in a line across the wrap and top with the avocado pieces.

slice the tomatoes and lay them on top of the line of other ingredients.

roll up tightly and pin in place with cocktail stick (not essential).

package up in tinfoil and head on your way knowing lunch is one less thing to worry about.

hoisin crab wraps

4 x 10in flour tortillas

2 x 185g tins of crab meat

½ cucumber

4 tbsp mayonnaise

2 tbsp hoisin sauce

4 spring onions

squeeze as much brine from the drained crab meat as possible.

beat together the mayo and hoisin sauce.

spread the hoisin/mayo over the wraps, smearing it to the edges.

spoon the crab into a line across the wrap.

slice the cucumber and spring onion into strips and arrange on top of the crab.

roll the wrap up tightly and pin in place with a cocktail stick (not essential).

package up in tinfoil ready for your journey.

apricot and ginger gratin

Puddings. For most students these post-meal delights become a rare treat at uni. You may think you haven't got the time or the money for a sweet. Well as innovators of the student cooking world we're putting an end to this dearth of desserts right now, so chuck your shoddy excuses down the drain and cook up these little beauties. They're cheap, tasty and quick to prepare.

tin of apricot halves in syrup (400g)
cream cheese (200g)
2 tbsp icing sugar
dash of vanilla essence
couple of sprigs of fresh mint, chopped
½ pack of ginger nut biscuits

drain the apricots and arrange on a shallow baking dish.
beat together the cream cheese, sugar, vanilla and mint.
spoon a dollop of cheese mix onto each apricot half.
bash the biscuits to a coarse crumb and sprinkle over the cream cheese.
bake at 180°C for 5-10 minutes until the cheese begins to ooze.

serves ❹
£0.60 per portion
5 mins prep ■ 10 mins cooking

chunky chocolate brownies

Picture the scene: you're woken by childish laughter and cheering. Party poppers scatter your uni corridor. This can only mean one thing – it's your mate's birthday and you've forgotten. Oh @#%! Your Sunday lie-in together with your goldfish memory has cost you, and what's more the shops are shut. Never fear, these brownies will save the day. A cheat's version of the kids' fave, it involves no complex baking manoeuvres and the secret ingredient (banana) will keep it moist for days. When you take it out of the oven they'll be eating out of the palm of your hands.

dark chocolate (175g)

butter (175g)

2 ripe bananas

2 eggs

self-raising flour (120g)

caster sugar (120g)

fistful of pecans

preheat oven to 175°C.

snap chocolate into a plastic bowl and add the butter.

melt in the microwave – TAKE CARE not to overheat it or it'll split (see Top Tip).

peel and mash the bananas into a large mixing bowl, then beat in the eggs.

sieve the flour into the eggy mix with the sugar and a pinch of salt.

spill the chocolatey butter into the mixture and combine.

lob in the pecan nuts, mix and pop it all into a greased rectangular pan.

bake on the middle shelf of the oven for 30 minutes.

wait before eating – let it cool for 30 minutes to firm up.

turn out cut and serve.

serves ⑫
£0.30 per portion
10 mins prep ■ 30 mins cooking

TOP TIP

Be careful – you can make or break this dish during the melting process. Keep the chocolate silky smooth by putting it into the microwave and take it out after 30 seconds or so to continue to melt with residual heat. You'll know if you've split the chocolate when the mixture looks like someone has chundered in it. Start again, sunshine.

lemon and blackcurrant fool

Nothing beats a well-deserved lazy night in to break up the usual slog of reading, assignments and hard-core sports training sessions. A DVD marathon to die for fits the bill perfectly. And let's be honest, every student has a sickly sweet tooth. So why not try a bowl of Ben and Jamie's lemon and blackcurrant fool. It's a gloriously satisfying substitute for a tub of your favourite American ice cream. Far less likely to put pressure on your arteries or your bank balance yet ideal to cosy up with as the credits start rolling.

cup of natural yoghurt [150ml]
cup of crème fraîche [150ml]
⅓ jar of lemon curd (100g)
tin of blackcurrants in syrup (400g)
2 tbsp icing sugar
¼ packet of HobNobs biscuits

beat the yoghurt, crème fraîche, lemon curd and icing sugar together in bowl.

crumble up the biscuits into small chunks and stir through the mix (leave some aside to garnish the top with later).

drain the blackcurrants and stir half of them through the mix. Do not mix completely, to create a marbled effect.

layer the yoghurt mix into serving glasses with the rest of the blackcurrants and finish with more HobNobs pieces.

serves ❹
£1.00 per portion
6 mins prep

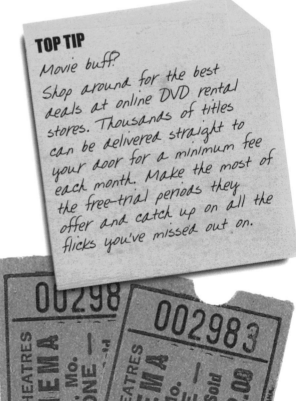

TOP TIP

Movie buff? Shop around for the best deals at online DVD rental stores. Thousands of titles can be delivered straight to your door for a minimum fee each month. Make the most of the free-trial periods they offer and catch up on all the flicks you've missed out on.

tips and tricks

Bring lots of photos and posters to pin up on your walls. It eases you into the process of being away from family and friends and makes you feel a lot better on those cold, rainy days.

Invest in a sound system. Crank it up on your first day and students will swarm to your door like dung beetles around the proverbial poo. It's a guaranteed ice-breaker, friend maker and hip shaker. Just make sure you choose your music carefully as first impressions last a lifetime.

Awkward silences. They're called that for a reason and can spread like the plague on your first day. The solution? Bring a shedload of booze, tea, coffee and snacks and offer them out to your new flatmates... it's your ticket to a talking point.

Make mates *before* you go to uni. Join your online university forum; these groups will often tell you who's in your halls, so it's a great way to mingle in cyberspace. A little effort in the summer will go a long way during fresher's week.

Second year accommodation. Make as many mates as you can in your first year so that when it comes to choosing who you wanna live with in the second you have options and aren't stuck with the weirdo who eats his toenails. Check out your student union for housing info.

Discount cards

There are plenty of companies that offer student discounts and irresistible freebies. They may not be obvious so why not be cheeky and simply ask for one. It's worth a punt.

With age comes wisdom. It really is true. Be aware of this fact and get chummy with second and third year students. These veterans will be clued up with news on all the best pubs and clubs as well as other priceless uni advice such as where to shop, what to look out for, and so on.

Teams and socials. No matter how cool you thought you were in school, no one at uni cares. Rescue your reputation and join as many societies, clubs and sports teams as you can during fresher's week. You'll have the time of your life with the mates you make in these groups once the 'getting to know you' period is over.

Fire alarms. Don't even think about setting them off 'for a laugh'. It's not funny, and it could prove fatal. Genuine fire drills are a student's worst nightmare: waking up in the night in your pj's and trekking out into the cold is about as amusing as a rectal examination. So stay prepared and grab an extra layer to keep warm if the worst does happen.

Facebook. MySpace. Bebo. Even your gran has heard of these social networking sites. So for a heads-up we recommend making the most of these web hubs for sending party invites, revising and, of course, making new friends.

RECIPES

* beef stir fry

* it's nacho time

* build your own pizza

* stuffed mushroom

  * toad-in-the-hole

the mission...

'Challenging the Student Diet'

When we, as members of the **SORTED** team, look back on our first few weeks, we smile like the fat kid who's shot-gunned the last cake. Amid the relentless demonstrations of debauchery, shamelessness and outright depravity, we were naively tricked into believing we were the superhero students. However, we have to admit that after the plague of Fresher's flu hit and the novelty of building pizza box towers wore thin we conceded defeat to a healthier way of living.

During a semester break reunion at our local, we were all fed up with the joke that our bodies had become. With this in mind, we were inspired to create the **SORTED** survival guide. Along the journey, the **SORTED** crew have set out to prove that a daily kebab can be substituted by a list of tasty alternatives which will save your GP from having a fit. What's more, the money saved from cooking your own meals means you don't have to be labelled as the 'tight git' of the group when you're next out on the lash.

As the miles clocked up on our **SORTED** tour, we managed to gain the support of other students, who are also fed up of sifting through the ready meal aisle every week. This final chapter is a testament to these junk food converters, as they present to you their favourite tips, tricks and dishes. We hope you enjoy their recommendations enough to preach the **SORTED** philosophy to your mates. Remember, **SORTED** is more than just a student survival guide; it's a religion...

RTED

look out for us on the road,
'Challenging the student diet'

beef stir fry

Attaching a red flag to your belt whilst you slag off a bull. Giving Mr T a nipple-cripple in a room with no door. Going to Oxford University. All very stressful situations. Packed into eight-week terms, students enter a world filled with college parties and bottomless pits of work, leaving them barely enough time to make their next Pot Noodle.

However, one man has pulled through, and his name is Lewis Iwu. Currently addressed as Mr President, he is gifted with the abilities of a Time Lord. Somehow, Lewis has found a moment to share his quick and easy stir-fry recipe. He suggests blasting some leftover meat, veg and noodles in a wok and before you know it you'll be staring at a tasty dish quicker than Michael Jackson can touch his crotch. This is a Thriller...

large beef steak (rump or sirloin) 200g

onion

1 clove garlic

thumb sized piece of ginger

red pepper

handful of mangetout

half a courgette

150g medium egg noodles

shot of veg oil

shot of soy sauce

dollop of oyster sauce

heat a wok or large pan on the hob and bring a small pan of salted water to the boil for the noodles.

crush the garlic. Peel and slice the onion and ginger.

cut the pepper, courgette, mangetout and beef into thin strips.

heat the oil in the wok and flash fry the beef until browned. Remove from pan and place on plate.

fry all the vegetables, starting with the onion, garlic and ginger.

boil noodles in the salted water according to packet instructions – usually 3-4 minutes.

return beef to wok with soy sauce and oyster sauce and drained noodles.

toss them in before serving with optional sprinkling of toasted sesame seeds or finely sliced chilli.

Serves ❷
£2.60 per portion
10 mins prep ■ 10 mins cooking

it's nacho time

Loughborough University is the Alton Towers of the academic world. That is, a LOT of fun. Elite sports stars, O.C. jocks, chic geeks... this is one place where you wanna keep your cool. This crazy campus uni is a playground that excretes fun by the bucket load. With fancy dress riots, the fun never stops. So keep your energy levels annoyingly high and indulge in some quick party food.

Georgie 'the chatterbox' Payne's special snack fits the bill perfectly. An exotic nacho platter accompanied by a truckload of dunk-able dips all loaded with melted cheese. What better way to stock up on your calorie count whilst lining your stomach for the mayhem to follow?

the basics
big bag of tortilla chips
wedge of hard cheese (Monterey Jack or cheddar)
jalapeño chillies
sour cream

peel and finely dice the onion, chilli, tomato, garlic and coriander.
mix together with salt, pepper, sugar and lime juice.
mash the avocado flesh and combine with all other guacamole ingredients.
scatter a large plate with tortilla chips.
grate over a generous helping of cheese and fling on some chopped jalapeños.
heat in microwave or under a low heat grill to melt the cheese.
dollop with sour cream, salsa and guacamole and let everyone dive in and graze.

Serves half a dozen partygoers
£1.20 per portion
20 mins prep ■ 2 mins cooking

tomato salsa
handful of ripe tomatoes
red onion
clove of garlic
red chilli
half a lime
sprinkle of fresh coriander
salt and pepper
pinch of sugar

guacamole
3 ripe avocadoes
juice of a lemon
clove of garlic, crushed
2 diced tomatoes
pinch of cayenne pepper
salt and pepper

Georgie Payne

LOUGHBOROUGH
STUDENTS
UNION
'Better Student Life'
www.lufbra.net

fancy dress is a must!
whatever, whenever,
where ever

build your own pizza

Let us introduce Bristol University Union's Tobin. An environmentalist at heart, he makes sure green issues come first, even if it means being chained starkers to a mighty oak tree at 3am. Okay, **SORTED** may have exaggerated there. But on a serious note, his union have introduced an epic gathering suitably entitled 'Well Wednesdays', where each week students are offered services such as free sexual/health (delete as appropriate) checks, fruit etc to promote their own wellbeing.

And his pizza dish embodies this ideology. Instead of forking out for a Domino's and caking each slice in the free sauce why not save some dollar and make your own? Whip up some bases, toss on some toppings and launch into the oven. A surefire way to take some money back off Mario at your local pizza joint and have you laughing all the way to the pub...

dough
plain flour (500g)
4 tbsp olive oil
tsp salt
lukewarm water (approx 250ml)
2 tsp dried yeast (best found in sachets)
½ tsp sugar

tomato base
onion, finely diced
2 cloves garlic, crushed
tin of chopped tomatoes
tbsp mixed dried herbs

mix the yeast, sugar and roughly a quarter of the warm water in a bowl and leave for 10 mins.

sieve flour into another bowl adding oil and salt.

pour in the yeast mixture and enough of the left over warm water to bind the ingredients.

knead until you have a smooth dough.

cover the dough with a clean cloth and leave the yeast to do its magic for about an hour.

sweat the onion and garlic in a pan with a lid until translucent.

dump in the tomatoes and herbs and simmer for half an hour to reduce consistency.

break off a quarter of the dough and roll out to a form a thin base on a baking tray.

bake in a hot oven for 5 mins. At this stage you can keep the bases in the fridge or even freezer until you require them. Make a stash – a really handy supper.

spread to the edges of the base with the tomato, top with grated cheese and your choice of topping.

bake for 10-15 mins in a hot oven until golden and crisp.

Serves ❹
£1.40 a pizza (based on ham and mushroom)
70 mins prep ■ 15 mins cooking

Pic 'n' mix toppings

Lashings of grated cheese and a
selection of your favourite toppings.
It's up to you...

Tobin Webb

UBU
www.ubu.org.uk

Ed Reacher
www.subu.org.uk
B|U Bournemouth University

stuffed mushroom

Meet our man Ed; he's been there, done that and got the T-shirt. Bournemouth University is his oyster, and he's got the nickname 'pinthead' to prove it. Where many men quake at the prospect of cooking, Ed is quick to shrug off any nerves. Together with Izzy and Christine, the team have spearheaded an online campaign for healthy student eating on a budget, getting more hits than a Paris Hilton porn clip.

Not only can these guys talk a good game, their dish proves they can be little maestros in the domestic arena as well. Their recipe combines a galaxy of textures and flavours nestled inside a spaceship sized mushroom, which tastes spot-on with a side of bread or salad. A taste bud orgasm waiting to happen …

2 large flat field mushrooms

knob of butter

dollop of garlic and herb cream cheese

couple of spring onions, finely sliced

sprinkle of chilli flakes

4 rashers of bacon

ciabatta loaf, halved horizontally

bowl of crisp salad leaves

splash of salad dressing

preheat oven to 200°C.

break off the stalks from the mushrooms and peel away any excess skin.

rub the base of the mushroom with butter and season.

cream together the cheese, spring onion and chilli and spread into the cap of the mushroom.

bake for 10-15 minutes until the mushroom has softened.

grill the bacon until crispy and then pile 'em on top of the oozing cheese.

toast the bread under the grill.

serve mushroom on top of bread, with dressed side salad.

serves ❷

£2.00 Per portion

10 mins prep ■ 15 mins cooking

KCLSU team

kclsu

www.kclsu.org

toad-in-the-hole

Oliver Twist, Del Boy and Jack the Ripper. .. these guys knew London like the back of their hand. So follow in their footsteps and accrue some insider knowledge by wandering the backstreets. If you're lucky you may even discover a local market. The Kings College London Student Union (KCSLU) certainly recommend these treasure coves, as the food here is a lot cheaper, fresher and healthier than your bog standard microwave meal. What's more, if you're clever and cheeky you'll befriend the stallholders. It never hurts to tell the butcher you like his bendy sausages, 'cos next time he may even give you a longer one.

After a bargain-hunt shopping session, the KCSLU team suggest a British classic of toad-in-the-hole. Utilise that sausage, smother it in gravy and lap it up with some mash and veg. Comfort food, cheap as chips.

12 herby pork sausages
2 red onions
level cup of plain flour
level cup of milk
level cup of beaten egg
warm vegetable stock - made by dissolving 1 cube (500ml)
tsp mustard
tbsp worcestershire sauce
tbsp plain flour

preheat oven to 220°C.

prick the sausages and scatter onto baking tray. Roast in oven for 10 mins until golden.

slice the onions and fry off in a saucepan to form the base of the gravy.

whisk together the cup of egg, flour and milk until it forms a smooth batter and season.

add 4 tablespoons of oil into baking tray with the sausages and heat up on the hob until the oil shimmers (*always stick on the extraction fans for this!*)

pour the batter around the sausages (you should hear a good sizzle) and place entire tray straight into hot oven for 25-30 minutes until the Yorkshire pudding batter has risen and set. (*Avoid opening the oven too early as this can make the batter sink.*)

stir the mustard, Worcestershire sauce and flour into the onions and gradually add the vegetable stock, whisking continually. Bring to the boil and simmer for 5 mins.

serve a substantial wedge of toad-in-the-hole with a dollop of mash and steamed or boiled seasonal veg before smothering in your cracking onion gravy!

serves ❹
£1.40 per portion (including mash and veg)
5 mins prep ■ 40 mins cooking

index

index cont...

starring...

Adam W

Ben Ebbrell

Tom Barnes

Steve L

Max T

Lauren S

Rich Smith

Tom H

Jamie Spaff

Jo R

Matt P

Beth

190

Jon Gavaghan

Dave O

Harry W

Liz R

Kirsty

Barry Taylor

James S

Charlotte K

Chris BM

Gabrielle

Joe P

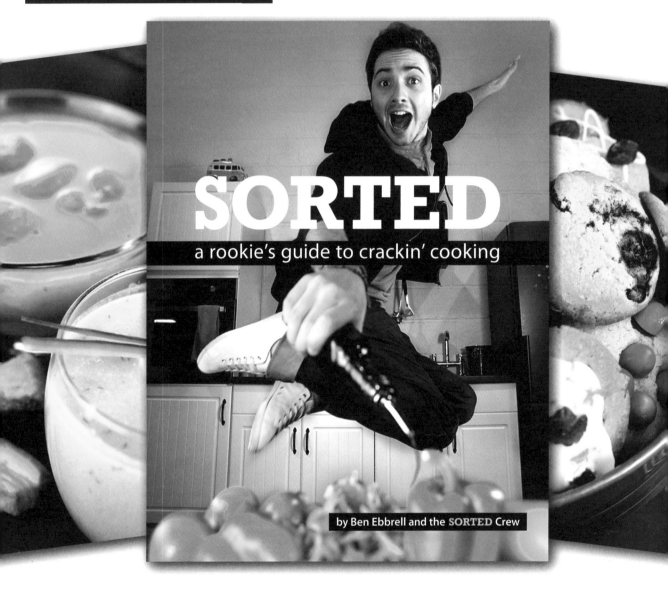

SORTED

a rookie's guide to crackin' cooking

by Ben Ebbrell and the SORTED Crew

"Encouraging young people to enjoy and appreciate food is a personal passion. I am delighted to support this book, it is full of great recipes for students to start their culinary adventure."

Raymond Blanc

"**SORTED** takes the fuss out of food. Instead, it makes good food fun, and is sure to get tomorrow's cooks into the kitchen today."

First News, the national newspaper for young people